Family FUN Book

Family FUN Book

More than 400 Amazing, Amusing, and All-Around Awesome Activities for the Entire Family!

By Joni Hilton

Voila!

RUNNING PRESS
PHILADELPHIA • LONDON

ACKNOWLEDGMENTS

My deep appreciation and thanks to the following friends who contributed some of the terrific ideas in this book:

Kathy & Alan Binder, Kathy & Dave Bullock, Liz & Lyman Dayton, Sherrie & Ken Hilton, Lisa & Eric Kline, Jamie Miller, Teru & Joey Miyashima, Christy & Ed Noll, Cynthia & Bert Rhine, Karen & Bob Rogers, Deniece & Jim Schofield, Nanette & Bernie Slaughter, and Juliet & Gary Stuteville.

Cover and interior illustrations by Jessie Hartland
Cover and interior design by Paul Kepple
Edited by Gena M. Pearson
Typography: Avenir and Providence Sans

This book may be ordered by mail from the publisher. Please include $2.50 for postage and handling.
But try your bookstore first!

Running Press Book Publishers
125 South Twenty-second Street
Philadelphia, Pennsylvania 19103-4399

To Bob, Richie, Brandon, Cassidy, and Nicole,
who definitely know how to have a good time!
I love you guys to pieces.

CONTENTS

INTRODUCTION

You're driving past a park and you stop for a red light. While waiting for the light to turn green, you look over and notice a whole family in the park gathered around a row of easels. Each one—even a little munchkin who looks too small to know how—is painting the landscape. They're looking at each other, laughing, smiling, having one of those quality-time moments you keep reading about. You feel a pang of envy, and as the light turns green so do you.

Then you think, "Wait a second, we could do that!" All you needed was the idea. You've got markers and paints and paper. And goodness knows, you've got kids. Nobody needs to be a real artist. And you don't really need easels, just something to paint on. So, next weekend, you pile the family into the van and off you go—making a wonderful memory and savoring life exactly as you always wanted.

That's what this book is about. It's filled with hundreds of ideas that will bring your family closer, knit your hearts together, and make life the fun it ought to be. Instead of spending your children's youth issuing directives, scrambling for backpacks, and dashing to appointments, you'll pause to sprinkle their lives—and yours—with joy and laughter. You'll establish loving traditions. You'll teach your kids to think creatively and to enjoy one another's company. You'll watch your kids become smarter. You'll even live more elegantly and create beauty without spending a fortune.

If "How can we ever spend more quality time with our kids?" is the question, this book is the answer. Some of the projects are from my previous book, *Five Minute Miracles: 373 Quick Daily Projects for You and Your Kids to Share*, and they literally take only five minutes. Others may take an afternoon. But they're all easy and inexpensive. And all of them have been lab-tested on my own boisterous brood of four kids and their pals.

Nothing you can do is more important than shaping the lives of your children. You're making their memories today. It's awesome and wondrous, but it doesn't have to be intimidating. Roll up your sleeves, slap on a ready grin, and dive into your favorite projects. There's something for everyone in this book and activities for all ages.

I applaud every parent who lets the phone ring, the grass grow, and the dinner wait while making time to enjoy their family. That's what life is all about.

*What You Won't Find in This Book:

DISSECTING

Please. I'm a wuss. No one is going to dissect so much as a gnat in my house. If you want to get "into" bugs as a family, be my guest. Science supply stores can provide everything you need. Maybe even the worms.

EXCURSIONS AND FIELD TRIPS

There are so many incredible places to explore with your kids that you could write an entire book just on super destinations. Right in your own city there's probably a candy factory, a newspaper printing room, a post office, a fire department, a bakery, a hospital, a zoo, a concert hall, a theme park, and who knows what else. But you can find these on your own and tailor them to your own area.

MAGIC

Maybe I'm just a klutz, but every time I've tried to master a trick—particularly those involving sleight of hand—I flub it. I even ruined a magician's act once when I tried to be his assistant and fell over the dove cages backstage, stumbled through the curtains, and fell out onto the stage. You're welcome to try magic tricks if you want, but remember that lots of magic tricks are expensive. And to a child, nearly everything is already magic.

SONGS, SPORTS, AND BOARD GAMES

These are easy to seek out on your own, and I encourage you to spend lots of delicious chunks of time in their pursuit. But I left them out of the book because they require intricate explanation, and I want this book to be full of the easiest ideas you've ever read.

STORY READING

This is one of the most important parts of childhood, so I'm assuming you already do it daily without any nudging from me. Don't stop when your kids learn to read on their own, either. Keep up the ritual right into their teens. It's a warm, cozy memory that all of us enjoy at any age.

*The Best Way to Use This Book

PLAN AHEAD

Glance through the ideas, pick the ones you like best, and jot them on a calendar. This way the goal moves from a hazy mental wish to a concrete commitment. If the project requires supplies, make sure you have them on hand. Often it's just a matter of finding the glue and string.

LAUGH AT THE FLOPS

And may you get many opportunities. Some of my kids' favorite stories are about the disasters—the gingerbread house that collapsed, the clay that wouldn't thicken, the fish that wouldn't bite, the centerpiece the cat ate. A sense of humor is a legacy you can pass on to your kids by spending enough time with them to ensure a few disasters.

TAKE PICTURES

Instead of a photo album filled with the same smiling poses, why not capture your child's wonder as she stares at a homemade volcano? These projects are also priceless photo opportunities.

INCLUDE GRANDMA AND GRANDPA

Help your kids make memories of their extended family, too. Spread the magic and watch how quickly love grows.

Spring

Rubber Cement

red

CROCUS

*Plant a Garden

There is something grand and wonderful about growing a living thing together, even if it's only in a few pots on a windowsill. Give each child one kind of plant to tend or one row in the garden. Teach him to prepare the soil, plant the seeds properly, weed, and water.

Consider a miniature garden in an egg carton. Just fill each compartment with dirt, press seeds in, and keep them damp. You'll get quick results with radish or grass seeds, and many flower seeds sprout quickly, too. *Hint: Start small. It's more fun to grow three tomato plants in a two-foot-square garden than to plant half an acre and get overwhelmed with the weeding!

*Camp Indoors

Beat Spring's rainy weather; go camping in your living room. Set up a tent or drape a sheet over a length of twine. Roll out the sleeping bags, tell scary stories, and sing campfire songs. Sneak into the kitchen to make s'mores.

RECIPE FOR S'MORES:

Place a square of a chocolate candy bar on a square of graham cracker. Top with a big marshmallow, then microwave for 30 seconds at a time, until the marshmallow begins to melt. Top with a second graham cracker square, pressing down to make a sandwich.

*Make a Backward Movie

Kids will shriek with laughter at this one. Choose a simple story line (an updated nursery rhyme works as well as anything else). Devise ways to do everything backward. When you run the movie in reverse you will appear to be doing it forward. (And fast, like an old-time movie.) Try walking, putting on a coat, jumping into a pool, eating, sliding, or throwing a ball to a dog. The possibilities are endless. This is guaranteed to be hilarious.

Afterward, award your own Oscars or Golden Globes. You could have a Best Supporting Dog, or the family baby could be Most Promising Newcomer.

*Create Your Own Walk of Fame

Recycle aluminum pie tins by filling them with plaster or cement and letting your little stars press their hands and feet into them, just like celebrities at Mann's Chinese Theatre. Save them for posterity or use them as novel stepping stones in your spring garden.

*Have a Movie Marathon

This is another wonderful rainy-day activity. Introduce your kids to the hilarious classics. Our kids howled with laughter at Abbott and Costello, Laurel and Hardy, and the Marx Brothers. Dozens of videotapes are available for free from most libraries.

*Make a Flip Movie

These are a blast! Draw a face in the upper right-hand corner of each card in a stack of 3 x 5 cards. Make the eyes roll, the tongue stick out, or a beard grow by changing the drawing a tiny bit on each succeeding card. You can draw a bud opening, a balloon popping, or a simple dot dancing around. Now staple (or secure with a rubber band) the left side of the cards, being careful to keep them in order. Flip quickly through them and your drawings will actually appear to move. Explain that this is how real cartoon movies are made. Encourage your child to make sound effects as she flips through the booklet.

*Conduct a Popcorn Taste Test

Pop up several brands and sample them as you enjoy the movies. Even if you know your preference, better make another go-round of samples, just to be sure! Take a vote and see which kind is most popular with your family. Look for the hybrid miniature popcorn that pops up with no hulls. Try coating the popcorn with caramel, or with dark or white chocolate, then mixing it with M&Ms.

*Make Your Own Movie Candy Bars

What's a day at the movies without some treats? Melt white or milk chocolate chips in the top of a double boiler over simmering water. After the chocolate melts, pour it into a greased mixing bowl and let kids stir in almonds, raisins, puffed rice cereal, marsh-mallows, or coconut. Spread the mixture onto waxed paper and let harden. Break into chunks to enjoy as you screen your movie together.

Or, try this easy-but-decadent recipe.
CHOCOLATE PEANUT BUTTER BALLS:
Mix an 18-ounce jar of peanut butter with a melted stick (½ cup) of butter. Add a pound of powdered sugar and knead with your hands until smooth. Form mixture into 1-inch balls and dip into melted milk chocolate. Place candies on waxed paper to harden.

*Create Garden Signs

This adds a whimsical touch to any garden. Just use wood glue to attach a 6 x 8-inch piece of plywood to a painting stir stick to form a sign. Paint it white. Now write "Mom's Garden" (or whomever's) in bright paint, adding a flower or a ladybug if you wish. Varnish, dry on waxed paper, then stick into the soil in your garden or in a flower pot by the door. They make great gifts, too.

*Hatch Eggs or Butterflies

Schools do it—why not do it right in your own kitchen? There are several ways for children to watch a metamorphosis. You can mail order a butterfly kit or contact local schools for information. Farmers often have fertilized eggs, and a separate project could include learning how to make an incubator box to help the eggs hatch.

*Be sure that you have a home for the hatched chicks!

*Paint Garden Gloves

Who says you can't make weeding more whimsical? Using craft acrylic paint, decorate miniature fruits, vegetables, or flowers on your garden gloves. How about a 3-carrot ring? This makes a fun gift, too. While you're at it, paint a baseball cap or a straw hat for the gardener to wear. And how about painting the pockets of an apron or tool belt that holds clippers, spades, etc.?

*Begin a Six-Day Series on Native Americans

Help your child gain respect for the original inhabitants of our country with the following series of activities. Schedule one each day for a week or spread them out over a month of weekends.

1. Make pottery. Many early Native Americans fashioned all their cookware from clay. Much of it is decorative and artistic. Here's a recipe for a clay you can mold into pinch pots or sculptures of your own:

1 cup cornstarch

2 cups baking soda

¼ cup cold water

5 drops food coloring (if desired)

Mix cornstarch, baking soda, and cold water in a saucepan over medium heat. Add a few drops of food coloring if you wish. Stir until mixture thickens and forms a paste. This takes just a few minutes. Keep clay in self-sealing freezer bag in the fridge so it won't dry out. When you're ready to sculpt, knead the clay until it's a pliable consistency. Let dry, then decorate with craft paint or shellac.

2. Stitch moccasins. You can use chamois leather, towels, vinyl, or heavy fabric to create shoes similar to ones worn by early Native Americans. The pattern is easy to make. Simply trace your child's foot on the fabric, leaving an extra inch all around. Now trace just the upper half of that same foot, and this piece will become the top of the shoe. Cut a long strip of fabric that's one or two inches wide: this will form the sides of the shoe. Punch holes one-half inch from the edges, then sew the parts together using yarn or leather shoelaces. Repeat the process for the other foot, and you'll have a quickly crafted pair of moccasins. (An alternative to sewing is using a glue gun, an appliance you'll wonder how you lived without once you own one.) You can then decorate the moccasins with drawings, or even sew on tiny beaded designs. For a real quick fix, make mock moccasins by decorating a pair of white socks!

3. Create sand paintings. Many Native American groups still make gorgeous sand paintings. To create one, collect various

colors of dry dirt and sand. (You may want to do this ahead of time, when you're visiting places away from home). Or, you can make your own colored "sand" by rubbing colored chalk against coarse sandpaper. Pour alternating layers of sand into a clear jar to make an interesting design. See if you can make yours look like mountains, a sunset, or a fun geometric pattern.

4. Make a miniature village. There were dozens of varieties of Native American homes besides the familiar teepee. Library books provide a wealth of information. Start with a piece of poster board for the ground. Your child can sprinkle sand or dirt over glue to make the ground. Now cut an egg carton into twelve compartments and make each into a kind of dwelling. Glue toothpicks or twigs vertically around one to make a Creek house or a Wichita grass house. Cover some with clay, brush, or bark to make various shelters and wigwams of the northeastern natives. Let your child arrange them into a village. Add a stream, a garden, animals, or a play area for children. Use a longer box to make an Iroquois long house (and read *The Indian in the Cupboard*). Your child will spend hours imagining in his own village.

5. Weave place mats. Many Native Americans wove fabric not only for clothing, but for sleeping mats and blankets, ceremonial costumes, and reed baskets. Weaving is still a treasured art today. Your project can be as simple or as elaborate as you wish. Cut construction paper into half-inch strips. Then place several strips parallel on a table and help your child weave over, under, over, under with another strip. Pick up the next strip and weave the opposite way—under, over, under, over. Keep going until you've woven a rectangle, then cover the mat with clear laminating plastic.

6. Eat a totem pole cake. This is so easy, yet so terrific when it's finished—you must remember to take pictures. If you wish, study ahead about totem pole symbols— the eagle, the salmon, the thunderbird, the beaver, the bear, and others.

Use a purchased, frozen pound cake. (They are easy to cut into shapes.) Let your cake thaw, then cut it into chunks. Prepare various colors of frosting and let your child decorate each chunk to look like a different animal. Don't forget tiny candies for the eyes. Stack them vertically if you can (or lay them down on a cookie sheet), and let your child tell you the story of her creation. We like to use two pound cakes to make our totem pole really high!

*Watch for the First Crocus

See who can be the first to spot a crocus growing in your town (or yard), then plan a picnic or outing to celebrate it. Have a special menu that's only for this grand occasion. Let spring waltz in with some fanfare! My father once planted crocus bulbs in letter shapes on our sloping front lawn, and when the snow melted, up came colorful blooms that spelled out "IT'S SPRING!"

*Keep Your Eye on the Sky

Spring is a great time for watching clouds. Talk about how they form from tiny droplets of water or ice crystals, and learn their names: cirrus (the wispy white clouds), cumulus (the puffy white clouds), stratus (the horizontally layered clouds), and nimbus (the dark storm clouds). Explain that many clouds are a combination of these four types. Look outside and see what kind are in the sky today. Do any have recognizable shapes? Older kids can make a cloud chart and record the kinds of clouds they see in the sky each day.

*Add a Touch of Spring to Your Kitchen

1. Hang bunches of dried flowers from coat pegs.

2. Use a flowerpot or a watering can (painted with flowers) to hold kitchen utensils.

3. Replace curtain valances with grapevines and silk flower garlands.

4. Hang a garden hat on the wall, tied with a fluffy bow. Paint garden tools to match your kitchen and hang them beside the hat.

*Make an Outdoor Topiary

Add whimsical fun to your landscaping. Bend a wire hanger into the shape of an animal, then stick it in the ground (or into an indoor pot). Plant ivy at its base and train the tendrils to wrap around your wire creation. Another idea is to clip a juniper bush into pom-poms, cones, cubes, and animal shapes.

*Design Your Own Umbrellas

Inexpensive, solid-colored umbrellas are fun to paint. Use a washable fabric paint and let your kids make their own designs. How about leopard spots? Zigzags? Raindrops? A sunny day? If your umbrella has sprung a leak, use tiny bathtub decals as patches. Paint an inexpensive slicker to match. (Comb through thrift shops and consignment stores for great bargains on new-looking raincoats.)

*Let Kids Do Spring Cleaning, Too

Make up "Kid Cleaning Kits." Look for small sponges, rags, brushes, and tiny pump bottles of water. You can even find child-sized garden tools and gloves. Craft stores sell inexpensive children's aprons. Place them in a plastic tote with your child's name on it. Kids will feel like important members of the cleaning crew.

*Grow a Crystal Garden

In a baby food or other small jar, mix 1 tablespoon Epsom salts, 1 tablespoon water, and ¼ tablespoon food coloring. Set aside. Don't disturb the jars. Over the next few days you'll be able to watch beautiful crystals grow.

*Make Snail Art

Let snails creep through tempera paint on a sheet of paper. As they move along, they'll leave beautiful trails of color. Worm art works the same way. The paint won't hurt the snails (think of all the stuff they crawl over!), and afterward you can return the little critters to their nature home.

*Help Birds Build Nests

Leave bits of dryer lint where birds can pick them up. Other useful bits of fluff and string can be left on bushes where birds might gather them. This spring you might see a bit of red yarn peeking out atop the branches!

*Collect Rainwater

Rinse your hair with rainwater the next time you shampoo. Are the old wives' tales true? Does it leaves your hair softer?

*Freeze Rainbows

As soon as you see the first rainbow of a spring rain, make rainbow pops. Freeze layers of varying colors of juice in popsicle forms or in paper cups with a plastic spoon inserted. Some good combinations are a layer of papaya, apple, or peach juice, followed by a layer of grape or cranberry, and topped with a layer of pink lemonade, guava, or orange juice. Let freeze between layering. What a fun and healthful after-school snack!

*Make Liquid Rainbows

This is one of my kids' favorite projects. Cut a red cabbage into small chunks and boil them in a saucepan containing about two cups of water. Save or discard the cabbage; it's the water it boiled in that makes the magic.

Pour the purplish-blue water into several clear, heat-resistant glasses, mugs, or measuring cups. Now the magic begins. Add a spoonful of baking soda to one glass and watch what happens to the color. Now add a spoonful of vinegar to another glass—what color does that make? What color do you get if you pour the two together? Teach your kids that acids and bases account for the excitement. (Baking soda should create brilliant blues and greens; vinegar should turn the liquid deep reds and bright pinks.)

*Grow a Terrarium

Terrariums usually contain plants and animals (such as worms or insects) that exchange oxygen and carbon dioxide. But you can also make one that contains only plants. And they make wonderful gifts, too. Use a large, clean jar, bottle, or glass bowl. Spread a thick layer of pebbles on the bottom for drainage. Cover it with soil and tiny plants. Now arrange colored shells, driftwood, interesting rocks, aquarium gravel, even tiny figurines inside.

*Clip Your Own Bonsai Tree

Ask a florist what kind of small juniper to use. (Finished bonsai's are incredibly expensive, but a small juniper in a plastic pot shouldn't cost nearly as much.) Study how bonsai's are trimmed to resemble large trees, then carefully clip yours in the same way. Let your child clip, too, under your supervision. My father gathered the family around the kitchen table when I was a young girl and gave us each a tiny tree to work on. I still remember how proud I was to display my "pruning" to my parents.

*Grow Sprouts

Fill a clean, wide-mouthed jar with damp paper towels or a damp sponge. Be careful not to pack the jar too tightly. The towels should just press lightly against the jar's sides. Now insert some seeds between the glass and the towels. Good seeds to try are a variety of beans, citrus fruits, corn, peas, squash, pears, and apples. Keep the towels moist by drizzling water on them each day. Within a day or two, you'll notice sprouts and roots.

When the leafy stems have pushed up into the air, tip the jar onto its side. Within a day you'll notice that the stems have bent so that the sprout is still reaching straight up. The roots have also curved to grow straight down. This effect is created by a growth hormone within the plant, and the process is called *geotropism*.

*Hang a Sun-Catcher

Now that sunny days are approaching, you can enjoy the play of light and color in your rooms. Cut two sheets of waxed paper into the same shape (a heart, a house, a butterfly, whatever), and place crayon crumbs between them. Press the paper with a warm iron. The crayon crumbs will melt and spread into bright splashes of color. Don't separate the waxed paper. Instead, punch a hole at the top and hang it from a thread in a favorite window.

*Create a Parachute

Enjoy spring's breezy weather by tossing a homemade parachute into the air and watching it twirl through the skies.

Tie a knot in each corner of a handkerchief or scarf. Toss it into the air and watch it float down. We started out by tying small rocks into the corners and dropping them off our balcony. They fell like . . . well, like rocks! So our experiment didn't work very well, but the kids roared with laughter and had a heck of a good time anyway.

*Make Flying Saucers

Color the back of a paper plate, then fling it into a springtime breeze, like a Frisbee. Advanced artists can draw little windows with aliens peeking out. Plastic and cardboard lids work well, too. Have a contest and see which saucer goes farthest, curviest, and highest.

*Make a Barbie Cake

This is perfect for a little girl's birthday. Purchase or bake a tube cake, such as an angel food cake. Push the legs of a fashion doll down through the center, until the cake is at her waist, then frost the cake to look like the skirt of her ball gown.

*Remember the Tooth Fairy

At our house, the Tooth Fairy leaves coins that have been brushed with glue and glitter. In some homes, she adds microscopic notes on tiny bits of paper. You could even have a special pouch or jeweled box just for Tooth Fairy visits.

*Have a Hat Day

This is a fun project for a rainy day. There are lots of hats you can design, all of them easy. Decorate black baseball caps (under $5 at a craft store) to look like mini roadways. Using paint the color of yellow highway lines, paint a street with a dotted line across the visor. Now let kids glue three tiny cars onto their road. My youngest son gets rave reviews everywhere he wears his.

1. Make wacky hats from blown-up balloons and loops of clear tape. You will not believe some of the Dr. Seuss-like creations your kids will come up with when they stack the balloons and tape them together. Real giggly fun on this one (a great party game, too).

2. Make a sparkling crown from metallic gold pipe cleaners. They're inexpensive, bend easily into zigzags, and are much more comfortable than those heavy crown jewels!

3. Decorate green visors with big, jiggly eyes, and you can transform a little prince into a frog. Fun party hats can be created by sticking feathers, jewels, and stickers onto visors.

4. Empty oatmeal boxes make perfect stovepipe hats for the little ones. Round ice cream cartons, washed and dried, can turn into top hats for magicians. Decorate them differently and they can become African hats.

5. Calling all maidens of the kingdom! Look like a fairy princess. Fashion a tall cone from poster board, then staple or tape it to hold its shape. Attach a chiffon scarf to the tip.

6. Help your kids become waiters and waitresses, and turn your kitchen into a 1950s diner one night. Cut the flap off a white, legal-sized envelope, open it, and boys can wear it as a waiter's cap. For girls, half a doily glued onto a headband can become their waitress hat.

7. Purchase an inexpensive straw hat, and on Easter morning, attach real flowers to it to make your Easter bonnet. Use hot glue, florist's tape, or wire.

E·A·S·T·E·R

*Leave Carrots for the Easter Bunny

Did you know that, like Santa Claus, the Easter Bunny sometimes leaves cornstarch footprints on the carpet? Sometimes he gets the powdered sugar on his fur when he's making the candy!

*Decorate a Bunny Cake

Purchase or make one round cake and enough white frosting to cover it. Cut the cake in half and stand the two halves side by side, with rounded sides up, on a platter. Frost the cake white, so it resembles a bunny's crouched body. If you wish, cover with shredded coconut. Surround the bunny with "grass" made by shaking some more

coconut and a few drops of green food coloring in a lidded jar. Cut two pink ears from construction paper and insert them at one end. Use a red gumdrop for the nose and two pink jellybeans for the eyes. Shoestring licorice works well for whiskers, and a Hostess-brand "snowball" cupcake is perfect for the tail. Since most cake recipes make two of these bunnies, we usually give one to a neighbor to share the fun.

*Weave Your Own Spring Baskets

Kids can quickly create original designs using the green plastic containers that cherry tomatoes and strawberries are sold in. Give the kids strips of brightly colored tissue paper or construction paper. They're easy to thread in and out of the basket's spaces. Older kids can use real hemp from the craft store to create more traditional baskets. Fill them with grass and treats for lovely gifts.

*Make Chocolate Tulips

Use white, dark, or milk chocolate for these beautiful confections. Simply dip the round end of a blown-up balloon (the long, skinny kind works best) in melted chocolate, letting the chocolate form 5 or 6 "petals." Place a dab of melted chocolate on waxed paper, then set your balloon upright in the dab to harden. When chocolate hardens, carefully peel away balloon (do not pop, or chocolate may crack). You'll have a flower-shaped "bowl" you can fill with Easter treats.

*Try New Ways to Color Eggs

Boil your eggs before you try these fantastic and colorful ideas.

1. Dip eggs in beet juice to turn them bright pink.

2. Wrap an egg with a wide rubber band, then dip it into dye. Dry. When you roll off the rubber band, un-dyed stripes and criss-crosses will be left behind.

3. Wrap eggs in damp crepe paper and let dry. Peel off the crepe paper and see the beautiful textures and stains left behind.

4. Paint swirls of rubber cement over eggs, then dip them into dye. Let dry. Peel off the rubber cement. You'll see beautiful, contrasting swirls.

5. Use star stickers and paper reinforcers to decorate eggs, then dip into dye. Dry. When you peel off the stickers, little Os and stars will be left behind.

6. Make marbleized wonders. Fill a bowl with water, then drizzle an oil-based paint onto its surface. Slowly submerge an egg into this mixture, then lift out. This particular technique works well on blown eggs, too. (*See below for blown eggs.)

**Please note: This kind of paint is not safe for eating and may penetrate egg shells. Never eat an egg that has absorbed ink or paint.

7. Be sure to use brown eggs as well as white. They take on marvelous deep tones.

8. Give your eggs circular stripes. My son, Richie, invented this technique. Get an egg spinning fast, then touch a soft felt-tipped marker to the egg. Like spin-art, the egg will take on entire circles of ink.

9. Buy wooden eggs from a craft shop and hand-paint them. Spray-paint them gold, then splatter on ivory paint (with an old toothbrush) for modern elegance.

10. Use a candle to write on the egg before dyeing it. The wax will prevent the dye from reaching those areas, and a surprise message will appear.

11. Cover blown eggs with sequins, jewels, and ribbons.

DIRECTIONS FOR BLOWN EGGS:

To hollow out a raw egg, use a needle to puncture two holes—a small one at the tip of the egg and a larger one at the wider base. Hold the egg over a bowl to catch the whites and the yolk. Then blow through the small hole, forcing the egg's contents through the wide hole. Rinse the egg and let dry. Then decorate.

---

12. Glue dried leaves and flowers to blown eggs. Shellac and let dry on waxed paper.

13. Decoupage blown eggs with magazine clippings of Victorian ribbons and roses.

14. Decoupage blown eggs with torn bits of colored tissue paper. This creates a beautiful, stained-glass effect. Try overlapping the colors.

15. Cover a blown egg with foreign stamps for the stamp-collector.

*Make Lace Eggs

Dip lengths of thin, colored string into liquid starch. Drape them all over a blown-up balloon. Cover the balloon fairly well, so there are no large gaps. Set on waxed paper to dry. When fully dry, pop the balloon and the string will maintain an egg shape. Gorgeous! You could even cut a large hole from one side and use it for your Easter basket.

Thin craft string is perfect for these eggs, and it almost always comes in multi-color balls. It's available at craft and yarn stores.

*Create a Vacuum

Here's another use for all those boiled Easter eggs. This has been dubbed a "totally cool" science experiment by dozens of kids when I've demonstrated it for school classes. Here's how you do it.

First, you need an empty one-gallon glass bottle with a narrow neck, such as a cranberry juice bottle. The neck of the bottle should be just slightly narrower than a peeled boiled egg. Place torn newspaper scraps inside the bottle and light them with a long match. Quickly place the peeled egg over the bottle's neck. Because the fire is rapidly drawing in oxygen, it will create a strong vacuum and the egg will be sucked into the bottle with a loud thunk!

*Make Egg-Shaped Pancakes

Decorate pancakes with chocolate chips or candy sprinkles. You can also cut sandwiches into egg shapes, make egg-shaped cookies, and even serve ice cream in large plastic eggshell halves.

*Scrambled Green Eggs and Ham

Leftover Easter ham is no problem at our house—we whip it up into omelets and scrambled eggs. Inspired by Dr. Seuss, we've even discovered that you can dye eggs green (they take food coloring amazingly well). Scramble some up and enjoy a colorful breakfast!

*Fill Eggs with Surprises

Instead of filling plastic eggs with only candy, fill some with stickers, erasers, bouncy balls, marbles, rings, and coins. Perhaps some could contain clues that lead clever sleuths to a treasure!

*Grow Some Goons

Fill eggshell halves with dirt and grass seed. Draw a funny face on each shell. Keep them watered, and in a few days your goons will sprout spiky green "hair." This same technique can be used to grow natural grass in your Easter baskets. It's so much prettier than plastic hay and not nearly as likely to find its way all through the house! Line baskets with plastic, fill with dirt and grass seeds, and keep moist. Start three weeks before Easter, and your eggs will nestle in a gorgeous bed of greenery.

*Make Glove Bunnies

Stuff an old white glove with jelly beans in two of the fingers and in the palm. Fold the other fingers inside. Tie the bottom with a bow. Draw on a bunny face and whiskers, and you have a cute critter to put in someone's basket.

*Make Sugar Eggs with a Peephole

SUGAR EGG:

1 cup powdered sugar

2 ½ tsp. water

liquid food coloring

2 hollow plastic egg halves

FROSTING CEMENT:

2 egg whites

½ tsp. cream of tartar

2 cups confectioners' sugar

SUGAR EGGS:

Mix sugar and water in a large bowl until you have a thick, spreading consistency. Stir in food coloring a few drops at a time until you have the color you want. Thickly coat the inside of two plastic egg halves.

Let dry. Remove from plastic. Chisel a hole in the top of one egg half so you'll have a peephole.

CEMENT:

Whip egg-whites with cream of tartar in a clean, grease-free mixing bowl. When stiff, fold in sugar until well blended. Arrange a miniature springtime scene in the half without the peephole. Fasten the egg together with frosting cement. Work quickly, as this frosting dries fast (keep it covered with a damp towel).

*Make Springtime Cupcakes

Decorate frosted cupcakes by adding a nest of coconut and three jelly beans for eggs. Tint the coconut green by shaking it in a capped jar with a few drops of green food coloring.

*Make a Maypole

Even if it's just an extra-tall garden stake, you can have your own family maypole and weave a pretty design with colored ribbon. If your family is small, invite some friends to help you. And be sure the girls weave garlands of flowers through their hair!

This is a super family reunion activity that symbolizes the weaving together of all different people. You could go a step further and have each family's ribbons match their T-shirts.

*Deliver May Baskets

Load the children into the car and drive them around to deliver darling cups full of candies and trail mix on the first of May. Make handles on top with pipe cleaners, or thread strips of construction paper through strawberry baskets to create their containers.

MOTHER'S DAY

*Send the Kids to Grandma's for Mother's Day

Trace your children on large sheets of butcher paper. Let them color in their faces, clothes, shoes, etc. Fold and mail!

*Take the Party to Grandma's

We did this for my mother-in-law, who lives in Tennessee. We set up the video camera on a tripod and pretended she was right there with us. We cut her a slice of cake and offered it to the camera lens. Then we formed a conga line and danced through the house. We set the video camera in different locations and danced the conga out

of closets, out of the shower—fully dressed with our heads all wrapped in towels, out of the bed covers, down the stairs, and all through the house. It was hilarious! We had Grandma laughing 'til her sides ached.

*Make Heirlooms

Hand-sew old family photographs onto tatted or crocheted doilies. Lacy ecru doilies lend a gorgeous antique touch to the sepia tones of yesteryear. Use doilies Grandma tatted or crocheted, if you have them. Or buy them for pennies at a thrift shop or craft store. They make great gifts, too.

*Tie Fragrance to Hangers

This makes a pretty sachet for any closet and an easy gift for kids to make. Gather bunches of lavender or any beautifully scented flower that dries well. Hang them upside down in a dry place until fully dry. Now tie bunches of the stems to a wooden hanger with raffia or pretty ribbon. Hang in the closet and enjoy the fragrance!

*Make a Stationery Holder

Pick up a pretty cloth placemat for only a couple of dollars. Choose one with a contrasting back side. Turn up the bottom four inches, then sew vertical seams to make pockets that will hold stationery, pens, stamps, and glasses. Now fold the sides toward the center, in thirds. Fasten on two 12-inch ribbons so you can tie the holder closed with a bow. Great for storing a paperback, too.

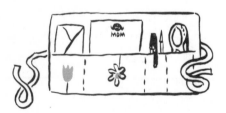

*Record Grandparents' Memories

Use videotape, if possible. Ask them what life was like when they were young. Find out what their own grandparents were like, what the best lesson they learned was, how they overcame difficulties, their best holiday memories, and their reactions to modern inventions. Learn all you can. This is a true heirloom (and copies make great gifts for relatives).

*Frame a Family Recipe

Not only is this an inexpensive way to decorate the kitchen, but it pays tribute to a "great-great" and the wonderful recipe they passed down. (I have one of my grandmother's English lemon tarts). If you can get one in the original handwriting of an ancestor, better yet. Mat the recipe with lace, if you wish. It makes a meaningful gift, too.

*Have a Mother's Brunch

Pamper mom (or grandma) with a brunch of her favorite delicacies. Use the crystal goblets and be sure to place a pink rose petal beneath each one so it shows through the goblet's foot and adds an elegant touch to the table.

*Frame Baby Clothes

Use antique or new baby clothes. Pin them carefully to a flattering background, such as a stiff mat or a sheet of cardboard you've sponge-painted or covered with pretty paper. Enclose it in a Plexiglas box frame. This makes a wonderful decorating accent or a delightful gift.

*Give Mom Your Heart

Soak a doily (just pennies, at a craft store) in liquid starch to stiffen the fabric. Ease the doily into a heart-shaped cake pan (with edges tucked up on the sides) and let dry. Lift out, and the doily will maintain the heart shape. Hot-glue dried flowers and satin ribbons inside, and you have a pretty wreath.

*Brighten Up a Hospital Stay

My friend Karen Rogers gets credit for this one. When our daughter, Nicole, had cranial surgery, Karen sent a huge box of little gifts for us to unwrap, one every day that we were in the hospital with Nicole. Each day we had something to look forward to. You could give a small treat, a box of pretty notes, or a whimsical joke—whatever your recipient would appreciate.

FOR THE PARENTS

*Celebrate New Life

Sometimes new life comes in the form of a brand new baby. Here are the ten best ways I know to ease sibling rivalry for the older kids when a new little bundle comes home:

1. Prepare in advance: Talk about the new arrival long before it arrives. Give your older child plenty of opportunity to see new babies, and borrow books from the library on this subject. Answer questions and share your excitement—it's catching.

2. Pin a note on the door: A note saying, "Come in and let Richie show you his new brother!" focuses the attention on the elder child, and the baby is now "his" to show off.

3. Buy several gifts for the older child: Tuck away wrapped, inexpensive toys so that when well-wishers come with a gift for the newborn, big sister will know she has a package to open, too.

4. Say, "The Baby Loves You!": Tell your eldest that the baby loves him. "And why not? You're such a neat brother." When the baby is old enough to look at the older child, point it out. "Look how he loves to watch you!"

5. Share feeding time: When it's time to nurse or feed the new baby, call the older child for "story time." You can enjoy an intimate moment with both of them, and the elder one will never feel that you're inaccessible.

6. Tell the new baby about the older child: Constant care of an infant offers plenty of time to chat as you dress, bathe, and feed your new infant. When the elder sibling is in the room, tell your baby all about her. She'll beam with pride as you recount her latest accomplishments and how proud you are of what a big girl she is.

7. Let the baby have chores, too: An older child may feel put out with the arrival of a baby. Suddenly they are asked to be more quiet, to share their toys, to wait their turn, to play more gently, or to fetch clean diapers. Devise ways for the baby to help. With your supervision, a new little bundle can lie on the toddler's bed for a few minutes to "warm it up so you'll sleep well." And a baby can be a "Presidential taster," tasting the applesauce, say, and letting it pass inspection. As baby grows into a toddler, he can be the accompanist on the piano, while the older child dances. It may not be the latest hit tune, but it will probably have a great beat!

8. Monitor attention: As difficult as it often becomes, it's still important to lavish time upon the older child and to have time alone with her. You don't want the new arrival to be associated with diminished love and attention.

9. Control behavior, not feelings: You may not be able to ward off all rivalry. But you can insist on a certain level of polite behavior and speech. Often a child who acts loving becomes loving.

*Give Children Different Colored Towels

Then you'll always know who left one on the floor! Monograms work the same way. You can carry this theme throughout the house. We bought plastic cups one summer in four different colors. Each child knew he had a color, and whenever a cup was left on the table, we knew who to call back and clean the area.

*Hide Coins to Teach Dusting

You can make a game of dusting if you hide pennies, nickels, and dimes for your kids to discover as they work. Or, hide buttons and see if they can find them all. Be sure to put some of them under knickknacks and such so kids will learn to move things and dust under them.

*Prevent Clean Clothes in the Hamper

Sometimes kids think it's easier to throw clean clothes in the laundry than to hang them up. Prevent this by charging a nominal fee for each clean item found in the hamper. Another cure is to remember that any child who can read can do laundry. Get your kids to do their own laundry and they'll soon stop throwing clean clothes into their hampers.

*Organize Shelves

Keep kids' books from tipping over on the shelf by placing them in an upright, open shoe box, one for tall books and another on its side for a longer row of short books. Several shoe boxes can even help organize books by category. If you wish, cover the boxes with decorative adhesive paper.

*Give Chore Coupons

Post a chart of extra chores that can be done to earn coupons, such as cleaning windows, whitewalls, patio furniture, or scrubbing and deodorizing the garbage cans.

Then assign each chore a value, such as two coupons, or five. When a child accumulates enough coupons (we used carnival tickets), he can redeem them for various fun excursions, a movie rental, or a toy.

*Throw a Baby Shower

There a dozens of ways to honor new parents and welcome their little one.

1. Have a couples' shower and invite dads to attend. Why should they miss all the fun?

2. For moms who have plenty of essentials, give a diaper shower. Everyone brings a package of diapers (or formula, if she would prefer).

3. Ask the new mother if she'd rather wait until the baby is born to have the shower. Many moms, especially if they've elected not to know the gender, prefer gifts tailored to the baby once he or she arrives. Also, she can bring the baby to show off.

4. Pass a blank book around to the guests and ask each person to write his or her best parenting advice.

5. Play some fun games. Remove the labels from a dozen jars of baby food and place the jars on a tray. Number the lids with an indelible marker and have the guests guess the contents of each jar. Later, write the answers on the jars and let the new mom take home a starter food set.

6. Time everyone for one minute. See who can list the most baby items that start with B. (Booties, bottles, blanket, bib, etc.)

7. Make a diaper cake. Fold half a dozen cloth diapers in half lengthwise, then roll one up like a sleeping bag. Cover with the next diaper, and so on until you've enlarged the circle and created the shape of a cake. Fasten it closed with a diaper pin, and decorate with rattles, ribbons, pins, toys, etc. (Even moms who use disposable diapers appreciate cloth ones for mopping up after little ones.) Place your cake on a baby plate and serve!

8. If the new parents haven't selected a name, ask each guest to write five favorites on slips of paper.

9. Give the *Family Funbook* book as a shower gift!

10. Give the new mom a coupon book good for baby-sitting hours, and give her a chance to have some time to herself or to go on a date with Dad.

11. Give the mom a basket full of things just for her—bubble bath, a loofah, scented lotion, perfume, cosmetics. Let her feel gorgeous again.

12. Give a time capsule. Insert the following into an empty baby bottle: The front page from the newspaper on the day the baby was born; a list of the current top songs, books, movies, politicians, and celebrities; one coin of each kind bearing this year's date; classified ads showing the current prices of cars and homes; a baseball card that might be worth something someday; and fad items that are hot right now.

*Make Masterpieces

Pack up paper, canvases, crayons, and paints, then take the whole family to a beautiful site and let everyone create his own landscape masterpiece. It's a terrific way to spend the afternoon and reinforces the value of each individual. You need not be an artist to enjoy this creative excursion.

*Paint with Water

Hot weather makes it fun to do art outdoors, and this kind erases itself! Let the kids take buckets of water and paint brushes out onto the sidewalk and create masterpieces. After the paintings dry and evaporate, they can start all over again.

*Curl Dandelion Stems

Ever since my first child held out a bright bouquet of these in his chubby fist, I have always adored dandelions and refuse to see them as weeds. Warm months bring them in profusion, so take a nature walk to collect a few. Be sure your dandelions have stems at least three inches long. Slit the stems into several strips by pulling them apart from the bottom end toward the blossom (the strips should remain attached to the blossom). Now immerse the flowers in cold water and watch the stems curl up.

*Here Today, Here Tomorrow

Do more than recycle aluminum cans; make a compost pile for biodegradables. It's a fun way to teach kids about the things we throw away and what impact we have on the environment. First, gather small bits of food, plastic, paper, cloth, wood, and metal. Bury each outside in a marked area. Over the next few weeks, some of the items will decompose and others will not, showing kids what biodegradable means. Which materials does your child think will decompose fastest? Which will not decompose at all? Now make your own compost. Using any size bin, alternate layers of dirt and organic material, such as grass clippings, leaves, and veggie scraps from the kitchen. Over time the organic material will decompose, mix with the dirt, and provide rich planting soil.

*Wear Ice Cube Necklaces

What a wonderful way to cool off on a hot summer day! Fill an ice-cube tray with water and drape a string over the cubes. Freeze. When you pop out the frozen cubes, they'll all be connected by the string. Kids love to squeal with delight when they wear these outside on hot days.

*Make Cool Clowns

Place a scoop of ice cream on a saucer, then top it with an upside-down sugar cone for a hat. Press colorful candies onto the ice cream for facial features, or pipe frosting onto the hat for ruffles and polka dots. Freeze for fun snacks. These make great party treats, too.

*Dry Summer Flowers

You can use the microwave oven to do this, or just let the flowers sit in silicon crystals for several days. Here's the fastest way: It's best to work with one flower at a time. Place the flower in a cardboard box. Very gently, pour silicon crystals (available in most craft stores) in and around the blossoms you want to preserve. Microwave for thirty seconds at a time. Carefully blow away the crystals to check the results.

Some flowers, such as yarrow, baby's breath, and statice, dry naturally in the air. A florist can give you some tips on which varieties to choose. Older children can arrange their dried flowers under a glass dome, gluing the stems to a wooden base beneath the dome. These make lovely gifts or decorations.

*Have an Old-Fashioned Taffy Pull

1 cup sugar

¼ cup corn syrup

⅔ cup water

1 Tbsp. cornstarch

2 Tbsp. butter

1 tsp. salt

2 tsp. vanilla

In a medium sauce pan, combine sugar, corn syrup, water, cornstarch, butter, and salt. Stir continuously over medium heat until mixture reaches 260°F on a candy thermometer or until a tiny droplet placed in a cup of ice water forms a hard ball. Remove from heat. Stir in vanilla. Pour onto waxed paper or into a buttered bowl. When it's cool enough to handle, you and a partner with buttered hands (this can be very sticky) begin to pull and stretch the wad of taffy. When it has a glossy sheen, lay it flat and cut it into small pieces and wrap with more waxed paper.

*Put Your Pillow in the Freezer

A few minutes before bedtime, let your child put his pillow in the freezer. Then, just as he's ready to hop into bed, he can get it out and put it under his head. Kids love the cool feeling after a hot day. The pillows don't stay cool for long, but turn them over for a second go-round. Enjoy it while it lasts!

*Have a Treasure Hunt

Take turns hiding a treasure, then drawing a map for the rest of the family to use in finding it. This can occupy kids for an entire weekend! Children love the mystery of clues and maps, and best of all, a surprise treasure.

Another twist on the same idea is to leave rhyming clues in various spots which lead the child to the next clue. (Each strip of paper says something such as, "Your next stop isn't very far—I'm hiding in the cookie jar.")

*Get Patriotic

Really celebrate Independence Day. Help your child draw a flag and tell her about Betsy Ross. Play some patriotic music and talk about why you're proud of your country. Make paper hats out of newspapers and march in a parade!

*Play Water Balloon Baseball

Fill all the balloons you can with water (you can never have enough). Pitch the water balloons like baseballs. Use a foam bat for little ones and modify the rules so that you win if you burst the balloon with your bat. Everybody gets wet and has a blast with this one.

*Declare Whipped Cream Wars

Go outside and give everyone a can of spray cream. Let the youngest person shout "Go!" as you all try to douse each other with whipped cream. The winner is the one least covered when everyone's can runs out. Swimsuits are an obvious must. Hose off afterward!

*Make a Beautiful Summer Centerpiece

Cut the top off an empty, clean milk carton. Place a tall, 2-inch wide candle inside, then fill with water. Make sure the water level is about an inch below the wick. Tuck leaves and flowers into the water all around the candle. Freeze. When you peel off the carton, you'll have gorgeous blooms encased in "crystal." Light the candle and place it on a tray to catch melting ice.

*Stage Wacky Olympics

Only include crazy contests that are sure to get your kids giggling. Include backward jumping, crab-walking, marshmallow balancing on one's nose, bubble blowing, feather tossing, hula hooping. The more ridiculous the better. Award medals with much pomp and ceremony, playing each person's favorite song as they step onto a box when they win a "gold."

*Go Ice Sliding

Nothing beats this old-fashioned trick for cooling off in the summer. Buy inexpensive blocks of ice from an ice dealer. Fold a towel and place it atop the block. Now sit on top and go "sledding" down a favorite grassy hill. Squeals and laughter always result from this old-fashioned way to have fun.

*Learn Something in Order to Go Somewhere

A fantastic vacation is always a great motivator. How about learning a foreign language before visiting a new country? Or studying an opera before attending a performance at the Met? Learn skiing in order to take a super skiing vacation. Take swimming lessons before white-water rafting, or scuba lessons before a trip to Tahiti. Study colonial history, then visit New England.

*Begin a Six-Day Series on Latin America

Tell your children that your neighbors to the south include Mexico and Central and South America.

1. Make a poncho. Cut a horizontal slit in the center of an old towel or a yard of fabric. If you don't have any fabric, simply use a large sheet of newspaper. Now make the slit into a T-shape by cutting a smaller slit perpendicular to the large one (this forms a sort of V-neck). Slip the towel over your head, and you have a poncho! Let your kids paint or color it brightly to look more authentic. Real ones are made from wool blankets and are worn mostly by villagers in the cold mountain areas.

2. Learn about parrots. Help your children draw a parrot on a sheet of paper. Then glue on some bright feathers. (These can be purchased in a craft store or simply made from pieces of colored construction paper.)

Discuss how these birds mimic songs and words. Ask your children to name other animals that live in Latin America. (Hints: exotic butterflies, monkeys, birds, lizards, snakes, and crocodiles.)

3. Make maracas. These are also called "shakers," and they make wonderful musical instruments. To make one, papier-mâché (see page 00) a small, inflated balloon. Make sure you leave uncovered a couple of inches of surface area where the mouth of the balloon is tied. In a day or two, after the papier-mâché has dried, pop the balloon. (The papier-mâché will retain its oval shape.) Pull out the balloon, pour in a few beans or some dried rice, and patch over the opening with more papier-mâché or tape. Paint or color it and get ready to make music!

A faster alternative is to put the beans in a can with a secure lid.

DIRECTIONS FOR PAPIER-MÂCHÉ:
All you need to make papier-mâché is diluted glue and newspaper. Here's how we like to do it.

Cover your working area with newspaper. In a small bowl, thoroughly mix a cup of water with a quarter cup of white craft glue. Dip torn bits of newspaper into mixture, then drape paper scraps on to an inflated balloon. The bits of newspaper should be one to two inches in diameter. (Any larger, and you will get wrinkles in the paper.) Cover the entire balloon with two to three layers of paper, except for a 1-inch hole where the balloon is tied. You'll only need to coat the balloon. Let dry overnight on a sheet of waxed paper. When dry, use a pin to pop the balloon near the knotted end. You'll hear crinkling and popping as the balloon shrinks, pulling away from the papier-mâché. When it's fully deflated, pull it through the hole and discard. Your shape is now ready to decorate. Paint with water-based acrylics, finger paints, or markers. You can even decorate with flowers, beads, ribbons, lace, or whatever you wish.

----

4. Carry things on your head. Explain to your kids that many people in Latin America (and the rest of the world) use this method to carry baskets of cloth or food, purchases from markets, and jugs of water. Borrow books about Latin America from the library ahead of time to show kids pictures of how this is done. Now let your kids try carrying household items on their heads—non-breakables, of course!

5. Make tortillas. Using just water and dried cornmeal, you can make tortillas, a staple of Mexican cooking. Experiment with the proportions until you can work up a fairly stiff dough. Pat the mixture into a thin disk. Now heat some oil in a frying pan and fry the tortillas. Sometimes they turn out like pita bread, which you can use for sandwiches, and other times they come out like crispy chips, which you can melt cheese over to make nachos. Either way they're a real treat!

6. Break open a coconut. Tell your children that coconuts grow in tropical areas of the world. I do this one outside because I like to use a sledgehammer! But before you crack the coconut, drive a screwdriver or nail into the dimples to drain the milk. Let your kids

sample it along with the white meat.

When you're choosing a coconut, shake it first. If you can't hear any liquid sloshing around inside, the coconut has dried out. Choose another!

*Make the Most of Ice Cream

This is the season for it, so here are some fabulous ways to dig in and have fun.

1. Make an ice cream bombe. It's easy, yet makes a dazzling dessert. Simply line a large mixing bowl with foil, then spoon in layers of your favorite ice creams, softened, until the bowl is full. Make contrasting stripes if you wish. Place the ice-cream mixture in the freezer until the ice cream hardens, then slide the foil-covered bombe out of the bowl and invert on a serving platter. Peel away the foil and slice.

A fun variation is to make the bombe look like a watermelon. Here's how you do it: Spoon softened lime sherbet onto the foil (and up the sides). This will form the rind. Follow with a layer of pineapple sherbet or vanilla ice cream. This will form the inner part of the rind. Now fill the bowl with raspberry sherbet for the melon. Press chocolate-chip "seeds" into the red sherbet after slicing.

2. Make ice-cream muffins. This is the easiest recipe you've ever tried! Just mix equal parts of softened ice cream with self-rising flour. For every cup of ice cream you use, mix in one cup of flour. Pour into muffin papers and bake as you would regular muffins. Fast fun—and where else can you find butterscotch ripple raspberry muffins?

3. Make ice cream without an ice-cream maker. Mix a 14-ounce can of sweetened condensed milk with ⅔ cup chocolate, butterscotch, or strawberry syrup. Then fold in 2 cups of whipped cream. Freeze in a foil-lined loaf pan.

4. Make an easy Baked Alaska.

CAKE:

8-inch round cake, any flavor

1 round ½ gallon carton of ice cream

MERINGUE:

4 egg whites

⅛ tsp. cream of tartar

½ cup sugar

Place cake on a foil-lined baking sheet. Place the ice-cream carton lid on top of the cake and trim around the cake until it's the same size as the lid. Loosen the ice cream from the container with a knife. Cut a 4- to 5-inch slab and place it on top of the cake. Place in freezer.

MERINGUE:

Whip egg whites with cream of tartar in a clean, grease-free mixing bowl until foamy. Add in the sugar until stiff peaks form. Heat oven to 450°F. Completely cover the cake and ice cream with meringue. Bake 1 to 2 minutes, just until meringue tips brown. Serve immediately, cutting with a knife dipped in hot water.

5. Make an ice-cream cake. Alternate layers of crumbled cake with softened ice cream in a foil-lined loaf pan. Freeze. Slice into a delicious, striped dessert. Try chocolate cake layered with cherry ripple ice cream. Or try angel food cake layered with strawberry ice cream. We tried Key Lime cake, and layered it with a lemonade-flavored ice cream and graham cracker crumbs. I call it Key Lime Gone Crazy, and it's super!

6. Set up a Make-Your-Own-Sundae bar, with all the toppings: sprinkles, granola, M&Ms, coconut, nuts, crushed Oreos, crushed mints, Gummi Bears, etc.

7. Put an ice-cream cone upside down on a plate. Decorate it with frosting and candies to look like a clown or a witch with a pointed hat.

8. Spread softened ice cream between two oatmeal cookies and freeze. Makes great ice-cream sandwiches.

9. Make ice-cream pie in no time. Soften a quart of vanilla ice cream, mix with a small can of frozen lemonade concentrate, and pour into a graham cracker crust. Freeze until firm. Refreshing and delicious!

*Play Hose Soccer

Have plenty of balloons on hand for this one. Instead of a soccer ball, use a beach ball or a blown-up balloon. One team tries to kick it over a designated line, while the other team tries to spray it the other way with a garden hose. Everyone gets wet, balloons pop on the grass, and a good time is had by all. (If you can hook up a hose for each team, it's even more fun.)

For another fun outdoor game, give each member of the family a bag of marshmallows to hurl at each other. You'll be laughing within seconds. (This has solved many a sibling squabble, I might add.)

*Play Target Toss

Real bocce balls are sometimes too heavy for little ones to throw. But this game uses Frisbees. Plastic lids are just as easy, too. Simply choose a marker and see who can come closest to it with their Frisbee. Or, design a course that each person must follow, and see who can be first to throw a Frisbee to each marker.

N A T U R E W A L K S

Nature walks are perfect family vacations. Here are some great things to do while strolling along a beach or lakeside:

*Make a Water Scope

Oceans and lakes offer a wonderful glimpse into underwater living—but only if you can actually look under the water. Take along an empty milk jug with the bottom side cut off. Cover the bottom tightly with plastic wrap, securing with duct tape or rubber bands. Now wade into the waves and hold your "glass-bottom jug" a few inches down into the water. Look through the top hole, and you'll have a snorkel-style view of underwater wildlife.

*Glue Shells to a Hat

You can make a perfect beachwear topper by gluing small shells to a straw hat or to a visor.

*Create Sand Art

On your travels, collect various colors of sand in small, separate jars. At summer's end, pour them into a large, clear jar in layers. Kids love to try to sprinke the sand in to resemble a sunset or a mountain skyline. Fill it snugly so the picture won't shift after the lid is screwed on.

*Make Sand Candles

This is another fun activity if your summer brings an excursion to the beach. Bring home a bucket of sand and pour enough water into it to make it damp. Scoop out the center to form a square or round well for the wax. If you wish, poke three inch-deep finger holes through the sand so the wax can fill those places and form "legs" for your candle. Now melt some paraffin. Add peeled crayons to color the wax. Place a purchased wick in your mold, then pour hot wax into the hole. If you like, top with sea shells. When the wax hardens, remove your candle from the bucket and discard the excess sand.

*Frame Your Memories

Nothing beats a favorite vacation photo, and the best way to display one is in a frame that ties in with the subject. If you have a great ocean shot, hot-glue sea shells all around a simple wooden frame or even a border of cardboard. If you went to the theater, surround your snapshot with ticket stubs, then varnish it. Line up tiny toy cars if you spent a long time on the road! Gather small collectibles when you travel so you can make a frame when you get home.

*Make Shell Barrettes or Earrings

Hot-glue your prettiest small souvenirs to barrette and earring forms (available at craft stores).

*Press Fossil Forms

Coat some shells with petroleum jelly, then press them halfway into cupcake papers filled with wet plaster. When the plaster sets, the jelly will allow your shells to slide out, and what remains will look like a real fossil. This makes a great paperweight for a student's desk.

*Use Sand Like Glitter

Let your child draw a picture or write his name with white craft glue on a heavy sheet of paper. Now sprinkle dry sand onto the glue and shake off the excess. Gorgeous! Do this one outdoors for easy clean-up.

*Have a Helicopter Race

Collect seeds and pods and see which ones will twirl when tossed into the air. Experiment with different sizes and see whose can stay airborne longest.

*Capture Sounds

Take along a tape recorder and let your child listen carefully for birds, brooks, breezes, laughter, squeaky swings, crunchy leaves. Tape each sound, then listen to them at home. Sometimes this brings back memories even better than photographs (and it's a great way to occupy kids on any vacation).

*Stencil with Leaves

Collect a variety of leaves, then lay them out on a large sheet of butcher paper or a brown paper sack. Spray them with paint and let dry. When you shake off the leaves, their silhouettes will stay behind. If you wish, use it as wrapping paper.

*Create Pebble Paperweights

Gather colorful, tiny rocks and place them in a jar lid. Fill the lid with white craft glue. The glue will turn clear as it dries, and you'll have a lovely reminder of your excursion. Trim the sides of the lid with ribbon or twine.

*Hunt for Letter Twigs

See if your children can find every letter of the alphabet by looking for them in sticks on the ground. Sometimes you'll need to put several twigs together. Can they find all the letters in their name? Take it home and frame it!

*Prove That Plants Travel

Look for various seeds and see if you can find all four types. Some are bristly and stick to animal fur to get transported. Some are seeds or berries that birds eat and later deposit in a new location. Another kind catches the wind, equipped with feather-light parts that keep it floating in the air. Still others burst from a pod, scattering in all directions.

*Build Vocabularies

Look for something *coarse*, *placid*, *symmetrical*, *glossy*, or *concealed*. Listen for sounds that are *muffled*, *incessant*, *resonant*, *melodious*, or *shrill*.

*Make Rubbings

Bring along crayons and paper. Place the paper over interesting textures, then scribble back and forth over the paper with a crayon. A picture will slowly take shape before your eyes. Look for granite benches, tree stumps, asphalt paths, and unusual leaves.

*Create a Topiary

Bring home tiny pine cones, seeds, or bits of bark. Roll a 4-inch Styrofoam ball in white craft glue, then dip it in your collection of tree material. Cover the ball completely.

Insert a 12-inch dowel or pencil to form the trunk. Now insert your "trunk" into a small flowerpot filled with wet plaster. Press additional pine cones into the surface of the plaster. Let dry. Wrap your dowel with twine and you have a beautiful decoration.

*Make Pebble People

You can even make them look like family members! Simply hot-glue smooth pebbles together to form people. Use three stones, piled snow-man style. After they set up, let the kids paint faces and clothes on your people. Glue the figures onto a found piece of wood or bark to make them stand firmly.

*Design Envelopes

Dry tiny leaves and flowers in the pages of a heavy book. When dry, place them atop the shiny side of a length of freezer paper. Small feathers also work well, and you can even cut tiny flowers from the pages of a magazine or seed catalogue. Now cover your treasures with wrinkled, pastel, or white tissue paper. Press with an iron for your child.

The result will be gorgeous paper that can be cut into envelopes (undo a standard envelope and trace it) or used as gift wrap.

*Cover a Box with Nature

Use an assortment of seeds and leaves to decorate a lidded box, such as a small hatbox. Use white craft glue to fasten them in a dense mosaic or pattern. Cover the exterior of your box completely. Great for holding trinkets, paper clips, or jewelry.

*Create Animal Characters

How many animals can you find in the park or the woods? Look for dogs, squirrels, even tiny insects, then make up a whole story about your characters. Your child might want to dictate the tale when you get home and illustrate it with drawings of his favorites. Will the spider save the day? Will the rabbit teach the duck to hop?

*Find Spider Webs

Spiders are nature's weavers, and their tapestries are sensational. See how many webs you can find, and watch as their makers spin their silk. Look for orb shapes, tangles, domes, bowls, funnels. Try to find some laced with dew—they look like beaded necklaces. See how many kinds of webs you can count.

Spray an abandoned web with hair spray, and it will stick to black construction paper.

*Picture a Fantasy

Your whole family can imagine a magical world. Read *Thumbelina* or another story about tiny fairies, then imagine where little elves and wood sprites might live. Can you find a tiny cubbyhole in a tree? What might they use for a bed or a boat? Could a nutshell be a baby's cradle?

*Make Chocolate Leaves

Bring home sturdy, non-poisonous leaves to create a delicious treat. Lemon, rose, mint, and camellia leaves are ideal. Wash them well, then dry them. Melt 6 ounces of chocolate chips in a double boiler over simmering water (or microwave for 30 seconds at a time in a glass bowl, until chips melt). Paint melted chocolate over the backs of each leaf, using a table knife. Place the leaves on waxed paper to harden, chocolate side up. Chill. Peel off the leaves and discard. Use the chocolate leaves as dessert garnishes or as delicious treats by themselves!

*Print Floral Fabric

Gather bright blossoms and fresh leaves. Place them on a board outside, and cover with a pillowcase or T-shirt. Now pound the shirt with a hammer, and you'll press the shapes and colors of the flowers and leaves into the fabric. (This works the same way as when you get a grass stain on the knees of your pants—you press the "dye" right out of the plants.)

*Begin a Seven-Day Series on Asia

Show your child the Far East on the map, and tell her that Asia has more than forty countries. It's the largest continent and has the largest population.

1. Fold a fan. Explain to your child that folded fans originated in Japan, around A.D. 700. They are often used in ceremonial dances. Here's how to make your own: Draw a pretty picture on a sheet of paper and fold it back and forth so that it becomes pleated like an accordion. Each pleat should be about a half-inch wide. Staple one end together to form the handle your child holds. Now take turns fanning one another with your creation.

2. Make a mosaic. First spread out some newspaper to make cleanup easier. Now pencil-sketch a simple drawing or design on a sheet of paper. Spread glue over one section of the drawing, then sprinkle on some rice, beans seeds, or noodles. Shake off the excess, and discard. Spread glue over another section of your drawing; this time, sprinkle on a new color or texture. Repeat the process until the mosaic is filled in. Explain to your kids that Asian artists make elaborate mosaics using these items, painstakingly placing each tiny detail with a pair of tweezers.

3. Practice flower arranging. Japanese flower arrangements stand out for their simple elegance and ability to direct the eye. If you don't have time to research this topic, you can still appreciate the beauty of nature's blooms and arrange a bouquet that's pleasing to your child. Encourage your child to vary the heights and the kinds of blossoms. Don't forget to include some greenery.

4. Eat breakfast with chopsticks. Cereal can be a fun challenge (but no fair sticking a chopstick through a Cheerio!). For more authentic flavor, use rice you've prepared the night before, or the kind that cooks in one minute, sprinkled with some soy sauce. Serve it in bowls and eat at a low table if you like, sitting on the floor. This is one time you want your rice to come out sticky.

5. Become a Chinese dragon. In China, the dragon symbolizes wealth and good luck. New Year's parades include a colorful dragon to keep the evil spirits away. Throw a blanket over your heads and weave through the house. Kids love being hidden under a blanket, and they'll have fun leading you through surprise twists and turns. Chinese music can provide a nice background. You can be a Chinese dragon with only two people, but the more the merrier!

6. Kick up your heals. Today, try some high kicks like they use in Korean karate. China, Japan, and Okinawa have styles of karate, too, but Korea's tae kwan do emphasizes kicking. Have your child kick into the air, and measure how high he can kick. Just as real karate students can earn yellow belts, purple belts, and so on, perhaps you can make up your own system of awarding colored belts.

7. Make a Japanese watercolor painting. Ahead of time, borrow a book about Japanese art from the library and show your kids some examples. Now create your own: Dilute some paints for a misty, soft effect, and use delicate strokes while painting a crane, a boat, a tree, or some blossoms. Older kids can try calligraphy.

*Display Collections

Summer is a time for long projects that can stretch over several days. If your children already collect something, think of a clever way to display it. One of our sons has a shadow box of scouting awards and a collection of nutcrackers in a bookcase. Even toy dinosaurs or action figures can belong on a special shelf in a youngster's room. Rocks, stamps, coins, cards—all can be arranged in a special showcase or box. My husband collects antique canes and walking sticks. Kitchen collections are natural ways to decorate—how about a row of antique rolling pins on one wall, or a framed display of menus from around the world?

*Record Your Kid's Comments

I've been doing this since mine were babies, and it's been one of the most priceless experiences I've had. Simply jot down their questions and cute comments in a notepad and keep in your purse. Every few months, type them all up and put them in a photo album (give copies to grandparents). You'll be amazed at how many comments you would have otherwise forgotten. And, through the years, this album has been an even better picture of their unfolding personalities than photographs.

*Hold a Family Carnival

Make it just big enough for your family, or be adventurous and invite the whole neighborhood. (This a great way for kids to learn about running a business.) Check with the local parks and recreation department—they often rent sturdy games, such as beanbag toss, ring toss, bowling, etc., for much less than you could make them for.

*Create Family T-shirts

It's great for reunions. Each family picks a color, and every member of that family wears that color. You can print your family name on the back or a favorite slogan or cartoon. These are great to wear to an amusement park or vacation site where family members could easily get lost. All your toddler has to do is look for the people in the neon pink shirts!

*Cool Off with Ice Dancing

Just drop an ice cube down a tucked-in shirt, and away you go!

*Hold an Evaporation Race

This is a good activity for a hot day. Place ice cubes on the sidewalk and guess how long it will take for them to evaporate. See whose guess comes closest. What if you put one in the shade?

*Start a Neighborhood Newsletter

Nothing unifies a community more than its paper! Your kids can become miniature publishing tycoons. They can do in-depth interviews with neighbors and gather gardening tips or jokes from them. They could even run a want-ads section. A variation is a family newsletter that goes to all the relatives.

*Hold a "My Favorite Book" Fair

This is a fun way to reward kids for reading during the summer. They can invite their friends to display a favorite book, then take turns doing book reviews for an imaginary TV camera (or videotape them). Dress them up as their favorite character. Have everyone bring some kind of food mentioned in their book. Another idea is to make books of their own. Younger kids can dictate stories to you, then do the illustrating themselves.

*Travel as Buddies

The buddy system is great for long family vacations. It pairs kids up with someone new each day and fosters unity as it teaches responsibility. (We've used it to erase hard feelings between family members, too.) Write each family member's name on a piece of paper. Each morning, designate someone to draw the slips from a hat, calling out the first two names to be buddies, the next two names to be buddies, and so on. This means teenagers help toddlers with their jackets and seat belts one day, then get paired with an independent parent the next. (Mom and Dad can even be buddies and stroll hand-in-hand for a change!)

*Play the Budget Game

This is not just a money-saver, it's a real vacation-saver. Give each child a set amount of money every day from which he must buy all meals and souvenirs. Suddenly, the kid who used to order everything under the sun (to get the toy) is now ordering a hamburger with nothing on it and a glass of water. (Do you think they'd do this if it were your idea?) Now he can afford that cool T-shirt or toy he wants. Gone are the endless hours of whining for every cookie and toy you pass. Either they can afford it or they can't. And any money left over at the end of the trip is theirs to keep. This will save you major bucks.

*Keep a Vacation Record

Besides videotape and snapshots, there are many ways to insure that your kids will always remember this trip. Have them mail postcards home to themselves, telling about all their adventures. Or let one be a news reporter, taking notes and publishing a newsletter when you get home—or reporting on videotape while you're there (a great gift for relatives). Have kids keep an illustrated diary or capture the sights and sounds on a cassette player. How about letting kids make up cue cards and put on a skit about the trip on video? Another good idea is to give children a disposable camera and let them take pictures. Often they'll capture things you overlooked.

*Project Excitement and Wonder When You Travel

Driving across a desert, Bob and I had so convinced our kids that we were in the Old West that when I dozed off, one of our sons asked, "You mean she's asleep and she's missing all this?"

And when a cabin's beds turned out to be lumpy fold-outs, I said, "Hey, look—you guys get to have Adventure Beds!" Soon they were competing for the squeakiest one. If you keep a sense of humor and a positive outlook, your kids will do the same.

*Play "Boss for a Day"

This travel tip will save arguments over where to go and what to see (even among adults)! Simply give everyone a day to pick all the restaurants and activities. By taking turns, everyone has a chance to call the shots and is patient when it's another's turn, because they know their own time will come.

*Begin a Six-Day Series on Africa

Tell your children that Africa is the second largest continent in the world, with more than 50 countries. More than 800 languages are spoken there.

1. Go Egyptian. Help your child construct a pyramid from clay or blocks. Older kids can study Egyptian art and architecture and the treasures of Pharaoh Tutankhamen (also known as King "Tut"). Wrap your child like a mummy and explain that in ancient Egypt, the dead were preserved with special chemicals, then wrapped with precious artifacts they believed would go on with them to the next life. The pyramids contained the tombs of nobility.

2. Stock up. Try some African food. Discover what foods are native to each country. You might even construct an outdoor market like the ones on the Ivory coast. Your child can arrange displays of fruits, nuts, spices, grains, yams, and flatbread. Other foods might include mint tea and pastries made with honey which are popular in Morocco. You can go "shopping" for goodies.

3. Make African art. Elaborate bead work, bright masks, colorful jewelry and robes, beautiful pottery and baskets, all have influenced Western art. Borrow a book from the library and show your child how to recognize some country's styles and motifs. Notice the brilliant colors and strong emotions in the art. Now it's time to try some of your own. Let your child choose what medium he'd like to try. (You can do the same with African music.)

4. Be a lion. Or a zebra, an elephant, a giraffe, a hippo, or gorilla. Learn about the animals that live on the continent, and let

your child pretend to be various ones (while you guess which one they are). Learn how they hunt, how they protect themselves from danger, how they communicate, and how they raise their young. Learn which animals are endangered and why. Can your child compile a book on African animals, telling a little about each one and drawing an illustration to go with it?

5. Learn Africa's countries. How many adults do you know who can name even ten of them? Your child can be a geography whiz by knowing them all. Write their names on a sheet of paper, then cut them into slips. As your child draws each slip from a hat, help her put them into alphabetical order. Or look at the list for one minute, then close your eyes and see how many you can name. The one who names the most wins. Another way to learn the countries' names is to let your youngster make up a song that lists them all, trying to rhyme whenever possible.

*Take a Talent Show on the Road

Kids can practice their acts, then request permission to present their show in two or three local retirement homes. Residents are usually thrilled to see young children, and kids love an appreciative audience! Involve neighbor kids if you wish. Besides singing, dancing, and playing an instrument, how about being a magician, a storyteller, a comic, or an announcer?

*Let Kids Earn Money

Kids can run a summertime business selling things they make. My second son, Brandon, even came home with his pockets jingling after selling rocks door to door! Richie earned his way to Space Camp selling stationery he had designed. How about selling bookmarks, potpourri sachets, painted flower pots, balloon bouquets, custom T-shirts, holiday ornaments, and magnets? You could even start a cottage industry selling nightcrawlers. (Can't you see your kid as a worm baron?) If your kids are artists, how about custom-painted birdhouses? How about a traveling garage sale—load a wagon with paperbacks and sell them for twenty-five cents each. One of my favorite ideas is to fill a wagon with water balloons and sell them for ten cents each. Nearly everyone would like to throw a water balloon and watch it splash on the sidewalk!

Chores earn money, too. Besides lawn trimming and raking, how about offering to photograph portraits of pets? Or draw a sketch of someone's house. Could a teenager tutor neighbors on the computer? Help older kids put together a baby-sitting kit (first aid, plus things to entertain wee ones) and make flyers announcing that they're available. Car washing, grocery shopping, leaf-raking, dog-walking, and other odd jobs can all teach kids about earning money.

*Clean Up the Neighborhood

This can become a summertime tradition. Race to see who can fill a trash bag first, gathering litter from your neighborhood. Teach kids about the environment and recycling. They could even collect newspapers or aluminum cans from local residents, and earn a little pocket money. Call your city council representative; maybe there's a wall that could be covered with a kids' art mural. Can you clean up a local park?

*Watch Falling Stars

Mid-August always brings a meteor shower. Find out when the best viewing times are this year and stay up late to make a stargazing event of it. How many can you spot?

*Hold a Science Fair

Invite neighborhood children to participate: each one can run a favorite science experiment for a few days, then share the results or demonstrate them. Set the experiements up on card tables on the lawn and let each child explain how his or hers works. Library books can spark countless ideas for projects. The local newspaper might even run a picture of your fair!

*Compile a Family Cookbook

Gather relatives' recipes at a reunion or through the mail. Copy old family photos and favorite family anecdotes and bind them with the recipes. What a treasure to have! Make several copies; you can be the first one finished with your Christmas shopping this year.

*Learn a New Skill

No reason to let our brains go dormant, just because it's summer. Why not let children set a small goal that can be reached during the summer? Some fun ideas: cooking a meal, riding a bike, polishing shoes, feeding animals, hanging a towel straight.
Let them practice until they've mastered the task, then present them with a certificate and much applause.

*Do Secret Good Deeds

Choose a day (or several) when you all devise secret ways to help others. It could be leaving a bouquet on somebody's doorstep, sweeping a walkway before someone gets up, or carrying in trash cans, but you mustn't get caught! Let kids learn the joy of selfless giving.

Keep a smiley-face mug in the kitchen; everyone can write down good deeds they observe others doing and store their notes in the mug. On a regular basis, kids redeem all their deeds for gifts from the "Smiley Store." Purchase inexpensive items they can earn.

*Have an Art Festival

Create art all summer, then have a festival to display the work for all to see. Invite neighbor kids to join in, if you wish. You might even choose a theme, such as "America," "Summertime," or "Let's Hear It for Kids." What if everyone made their art from objects found in nature? Could the art be donated to a local children's hospital? Remember, art can be sculpture, pottery, fabric—just about anything!

*Begin a Seven-Day Series on Polynesia

Tell your children this region includes Hawaii, Tahiti, Samoa, Fiji, New Zealand, and many other islands.

1. Make leis. Explain that most leis are made from fragrant flowers, but some are made from shells, seeds, feathers, and nuts. On many islands when someone puts a lei around your neck, they also give you a kiss!

Using a long strip of crepe paper and a needle and thread, you can make beautiful leis. To start, thread the needle with enough thread to form a long necklace. Sew stitches about an inch apart, right down the center of the crepe paper strip. As you sew, gather and fold the crepe paper onto the thread in accordion fashion; it will start to twist and form a column of color. Stack your crepe paper folds fairly tightly, and before long you'll have a great looking lei!

2. Build a beach. Polynesian islands are known for their dazzling beaches. Your child can create a picture of a beach by using blue paint for water, then gluing sand and shells onto the land part. (You don't even need real shells; cut tiny copies from construction paper or use macaroni shells.) Talk about how shells are actually the homes of sea animals. Have your child draw starfish on the beach, and explain that they aren't really fish at all, but echinoderms, and have no brain. Did you know a that starfish when handled or injured will often regenerate one or all of its arms?

3. Make a cucumber catamaran. Explain to your kids that these swiftly moving boats were once the Polynesians' only means of inter-island travel. They were made from wood and also used for fishing. You can make your own vessel with a zucchini or cucumber. Parboil the cucumber so it's easier to scoop out the seeds. Slice it in half length-wise and use a spoon to scoop out

the seeds and most of the flesh (use them later if you wish). Make a stiff paper sail and attach it to the canoes with toothpicks. Arrange the cucumber slices side by side and hold them parallel with toothpicks. Now test your boat to see if it will sail.

4. Make a fruit salad. Since this series is about the islands, try to use the fruits that grow there. Include chunks of pineapple, coconut, papaya, kiwi, mango, and orange. If you wish, serve the salad in a coconut or pineapple half.

5. Bang a drum. Explain that Tahitian dancing is known for the prominence of drumbeats. Authentic island drums are made of wood, shells, animal skins, and other natural materials. Consult your child about what household items you can use to make your own set of drums. Shoeboxes and empty oatmeal boxes work pretty well.

6. Weave place mats. Polynesian weaving is found in floor coverings, clothing, baskets, bedding, walls, and artwork. Demonstrate weaving to kids with long strips of colored paper or long narrow plant leaves. Place several strips parallel on a table and help your child weave over, under, over, under with another strip. Pick up the next strip and weave the opposite way: under, over, under, over. Keep going until you've woven a rectangle.

7. Make a volcano and finish the Polynesia series with a bang. Explain that the islands were formed by volcanoes and that many volcanoes around the world are still active. Here's how to make one: Sculpt a cone shape from clay, about a foot high. You can also make a cone from newspapers to form the body of the volcano. (Stuff this cone with crumpled paper to keep it from collapsing.) Fasten this "mountain" to a cardboard base. Be sure to leave a little indentation in the top, as this is where your lava will erupt. Now rest half an empty egg shell in the indentation and fill it with two teaspoons of baking soda. Make the lava by drizzling vinegar into the soda. It should foam, bubble, and erupt. This is great fun!

FOR THE PARENTS

*Capture Wedding Memories

Let's face it, the official photographer can't be everywhere at once. Why miss those marvelous shots of your guests? Instead, place an inexpensive disposable camera on each table and a note inviting guests to photograph one another. Have a pretty basket by the door where they can deposit the cameras as they leave.

*Make Moving Easier

Summer is the most popular time for moving (although a move during the school year can help kids form faster friendships). Either way, here are my top ten tips for making the transition:

1. Get brochures about your new town and plan some excursions to local attractions.

2. Fix comfort foods as soon as you arrive.

3. Find a great pizza or ice cream parlor and take time to enjoy your new locale, even before you finish unpacking.

4. If you're moving during the school year, ask your child's new teacher to have his classmates write a letter about themselves and what they like best about their town. They might even include some photos. And perhaps the teacher might like a "getting to know you" poster from your child.

5. Have a good-bye ceremony in your old home, reminiscing about the great memories in each room. This gives a sense of closure.

6. Don't wait for people to come to you. Go on a scavenger hunt to meet new neighbors. "Hi, we're the Jones kids. We just moved in, and we're on a scavenger hunt. We need a white button, a paper clip, and a rubber band." Chances are, there will be kids their age in the area, and their moms will call them to the door.

7. Let kids add their own decorating touches to their bedrooms, and make them special and uniquely their own. We let our eldest son splatter-paint his room, and you should see him beam with pride as friends walk in and whisper, "Cool."

8. Make a video of your new town's attractions and send it to friends left behind, along with an invitation to visit.

9. Give stamped, addressed envelopes to kids' old friends, so they'll be sure to write.

10. Have a special ceremony in your new home, making it official that a loving family lives there. Hold hands, light a candle, ask a blessing, whatever ritual you like.

*Keep a Busy Bag by the Phone

This can save many a mother's nerves during summer, when kids seem loudest just after the phone rings. Compile a basket or bag of toys to entertain them while you take a call. Don't let them play with the toys any other time or they'll lose their novel appeal. Some great—and quiet—items to include are pipe cleaners, scraps of fabric, stickers, paper, crayons, puzzle books, tiny action figures, and modeling clay.

*Store Car Toys Efficiently

I found myself straddling bags of snacks, toys, books, maps—you name it—on the floor of the front seat until I decided to divide and conquer. You can make a car trip infinitely more comfortable with these tricks:

1. Give each child a cake pan with a sliding lid. Inside, store pencils, glue sticks, paper, coloring books, and other items. When it's closed, it makes a wonderful lap desk.

2. Hang purchased or hand-made "shoe pockets" from the front seat's head rests so that everything the kids need in the back seat is hanging right in front of them.

3. Give each child a backpack in which to store all their "stuff."

4. Find a Tupperware or other container that will slide under the seats. Great for holding flat items, such as napkins or maps.

5. Pack a wad of wet wipes in a resealable plastic bag and store it in the glove box. You won't be able to count how many times you'll use them.

6. Dress the kids in multi-pocketed clothing, such as overalls. Let them carry their treasures right on their own person!

*Travel with Goodie Bags

Don't go anywhere without a large, resealable plastic bag for each child to ward off boredom. Inside, pack crayons, notepads, stickers, gum, games, aluminum foil for sculpting, lightweight books, origami paper, pipe cleaners, even snacks.

*Store Toys Out of Sight

Kids' toys seem to multiply overnight and get strewn everywhere. An easy way to keep children's rooms looking clean is to store toys in giant bins that slide under the bed. You can purchase plastic cement-mixing bins from the hardware store for only a few dollars. When kids are through playing, they toss their toys into the shallow yet roomy bins, which slide right under the bed. Now the toys are out of sight but easily accessible the next time your children want to play.

*Solve Sibling Disputes

Summer time seems to bring more opportunity for kids to get on each other's nerves and quarrel. Try these techniques for keeping conflicts to a minimum:

1. Send them to each other's rooms (or to lie down on each other's beds). Kids will work things out quickly to keep each other out of their space!

2. Put them on the same team. Tell them to go find a solution, then come and tell you what it is.

3. Don't allow tattling unless it's a matter of safety.

4. Put kids nose to nose to discuss a situation. Usually they'll end up laughing.

*Have a "Back to School" Huddle

Just like star athletes going for the win, stand in a giant huddle and give your kids one last pep talk on their first day of school. Some families have a special prayer—use whatever ritual you feel underscores your faith in your child to do well.

*Earn TV Time by Reading

Jump-start the school year by ensuring that your kids will not fall into the TV trap. To watch an hour of TV or play a video game, they must first read for one hour.

*Grow Your Own Socks

Walk in stocking-feet through piles of leaves or stroll through a nearby park. Let your socks pick up all the dirt, burrs, and seeds they can—the more the merrier! Place the socks in an open wide-mouthed jar, keep them damp, and set them in a sunny window. Watch to see what sprouts!

*Have the Kids Play "Stump Mom" or "Stump Dad"

To encourage our kids to pay special attention in school, we invented the game "Stump Mom." Each day after school, the kids would ask me a question based on what they learned that day. The object was to stump Mom, and the reward was pure satisfaction. It's also a great way to learn about how their day went. (And I must confess, this was a lot more fun when the kids were in the lower grades!)

*Make a Video Tour

Autumn is a gorgeous time to make videos. Simply go to a nearby attraction and let your kids be on-the-spot reporters, telling about the harbor, the zoo, the subways, the farms, etc. Make copies to save for Christmas gifts.

*Give School Supplies Some Pizzazz

Cover books with wrapping paper, newspaper comics, brown bags ink-stamped or decorated with stickers, wallpaper, a collage.

One of our sons found hologram paper and really wowed his classmates with his cool book covers. Cover with laminating plastic for extra durability.

Backpacks can be jazzed up, too. Let kids add their personal touch with fabric paint, patches, and iron-ons. Not only will this help distinguish their bag from a look-alike, but kids take better care of a backpack they've "created."

*Use School Photographs in Novel Ways

1. Enclose a favorite picture between two pieces of laminating plastic. Leave a margin on one side, punch a hole in it, and you have a personalized key chain.

2. Insert your child's photos into snap-apart plastic mugs.

3. Glue a small piece of macaroni to the back of each tiny picture in the photo package, then string them to make a necklace or bracelet.

4. Glue the tiny pictures around the rim of a small can to make a cute pencil holder.

5. Attach Velcro dots on the backs and use them as moveable labels on a chore chart, so little ones will know when it's their turn to help out.

6. Share them with your pediatrician— they can be taped onto your child's chart for easy reference.

7. Make them into Christmas ornaments. Purchase clear, plastic snap-together balls from a craft store. Cut a round of clear laminating plastic to fit inside, then stick your child's photo to it. Cover with more plastic, but this time a larger circle that will stick to the ball itself. Your child's photo will appear to float in mid-air inside the ball. Stuff tinsel behind the photo or fill it with objects your child likes this year. Legos would be bright. Snap it together, and it's ready to hang.

*Ease Separation Anxiety

Lots of little ones have a hard time being away from family members when they start school. Place a family photo inside the lid of her lunch box and cover it with laminating plastic to protect it from spills.

*Make Your Family into Math Maniacs

Teach everyone that math is all around us, and give your kids a boost in school. Here's a kilogram of great ideas:

1. Let kids drink from measuring cups one night, to teach ounces (metrics, too).

2. Purchase inexpensive little toys and wrap them up. Have your kids guess the box's circumference, length, and volume. Now in metrics. Afterward, they open the present.

3. Teach time by making your own sun dial. Just place a stick in the ground, surrounded by twelve stones. Make the 12:00 stone straight north. Then watch during the day to see where the shadow is.

4. Another fun way to teach time is to draw a giant chalk circle outside to make a clock face. Use sticks for the hands and have your child jump to various numbers.

5. Guess how many miles to your destination every time you get in the car. Toddlers can guess how many steps from here to there, right around your house.

6. Use fun goodies to teach addition, division, and fractions. Try graham crackers, marshmallows, or M&Ms.

*Make a Homework Box

We found our kids were coming home without any homework and decided to supplement. On days when they have less than thirty minutes of homework to do, they draw a 3 x 5 card from a recipe index box. I had compiled dozens of topics for them to research, a different one listed on each card. The kids type up their reports and also share them verbally at dinnertime.

*Make an Alphabet Video

Kids love to watch videos of themselves, so why not put one together that teaches them the alphabet? We did this for Nicole, and it was fantastic. She's the star of the show, pointing out things that start with various letters. Sometimes we even made the letters from clay or wrote them in sand. At the end, she posed in every letter's shape for a quick review.

*Write Your Congressman

As November elections approach, get politically involved and teach your kids to care about issues. Help them write a letter to an elected official—it can ask questions, praise good work, or recommend changes.

*Write to Sponsors and TV Producers

As long as you're making your opinions known, take a moment to write a letter of thanks to the people who bring you the shows you like—commend them for upholding family values. It is assumed that every letter received represents hundreds of like-thinking people who didn't write.

*Adopt a Grandparent

As weather turns cool, people get out and socialize less. Look around your neighborhood or church. Is there a lonely widow or widower who would love to be included for an occasional Sunday dinner or a movie? If your kids' grandparents aren't close by, consider "adopting" some for them. Invite them to your kids' plays, help your kids run errands for them. Treat them like family.

*Create "Homework Central"

Establish a bright, organized homework spot. Make sure you have all the supplies at hand, and let kids decorate the containers that hold pencils, staples, glue, tape, etc. Make it a comfortable place where kids like to be, and post a computer schedule to avoid arguments over using it.

*Make Leaf Rubbings

Create your own autumn leaves, even before the ones on the trees turn colors. Find several green leaves and cover each with a sheet of paper. Rub the side of a crayon over the paper. The leaf and its veins will begin to appear on your paper. Do your rubbings in reds, oranges, purples, and other autumn colors. Cut out the leaves and decorate your windows with them, or cluster them into placemats. Older kids can also learn to name the parts of the leaf.

*Play "Hot & Cold"

Hide a small object (in the olden days, it was always a thimble) somewhere in the room while your child closes his eyes. It must be in plain view, yet not obvious. Now have your child open his eyes (or come back in if you've sent him out) and begin to look for the object. As he gets closer to it, you say he's getting warmer, hotter, boiling! As he moves farther from it, tell him he's getting cooler, colder, freezing! Switch turns, as kids love to watch you search for something they've hidden.

*Discover a New Country

Select a spot on the globe or on a world map where there is no land. Then draw a small "country" on a sheet of paper. Cut it out, and tape it to the globe. Ask your child to name the new country and describe its weather, vegetation, people, and customs. He can even plan a pretend vacation there. Older kids can describe how the country is governed and how they solve their problems.

*Compile a Kids' Cookbook

Have your little ones draw pictures of the foods they like to eat and describe the "recipe" to you. Write it down below their illustration. The results are almost always hilarious (my five-year-old said to bake brownies at one degree for four hours), and a collection stapled together makes a wonderful surprise for grandparents, too.

*Make a Family Museum

Find a bookcase, a nook, or a cranny where you can display your family's treasures. Let one of the kids be the curator and write labels for special mementos. You may want to display artwork, awards and ribbons, photos, even lost teeth!

Be sure to rotate your exhibits, just as real museums do.

*Have a Hugging Contest

Here's a contest where everyone wins. See who can give the best hugs. Our family does this all the time, and it brings more joy into our home than any other project.

*Create Balloon Messages

Write secret messages on scraps of paper. Now fold them up and insert them into balloons. Blow up the balloons and tie them. Let your child earn the chance to pop them and read the message by doing chores or homework. Then she gets whatever the paper says (a park excursion, the chance to stay up fifteen minutes later, etc.). Another way to play this game—and this is great for parties—is to have the kids do what the paper says (sing a song, tell a joke, perform a cartwheel, etc.).

*Play "Penny on a Cloud"

This is another fun party game or fun just for two to play. Place a penny in a measuring cup, then fill the cup with flour. Pack it firmly, then invert it onto a plate. Carefully remove the cup: the flour should keep its shape, with the penny resting on top. Now, using a dull knife, slice off sections from the sides of the column of flour. Take turns, being careful not to slice too closely to the center. Whoever makes the penny fall, loses. (And tradition demands they pick up the penny with their teeth!)

*Make Hollyhock Dolls

Any other trumpet-shaped blossoms can also be used. Pierce a tight bud with a round toothpick to form her head. Then, insert the other end of the toothpick into the bottom of a second blossom to form the doll's full skirt.

Carved apple dolls are a treasured tradition. Though youngsters shouldn't handle knives, they can watch and direct as Mom or Dad does the carving. Peel the apple, and carve facial features on one side. Set the apple in a sunny window, and watch as it shrivels over the next few days. When it's good and wrinkly, pierce the apple with a dowel or hanger wire and "dress" with scraps of rustic-looking fabric. Apple doll heads are a cute addition to a holiday wreath, too.

*Make Butter

This is a great way to gain renewed appreciation for modern conveniences. Kids will never forget how much work it was to make butter from scratch. Pour a cup of whipping cream into a clean jar and screw the lid on tightly. Now shake and shake. This tedious job should surely be shared by the entire family. When the cream begins to separate, strain off the liquid and lightly salt the remaining chunks. Now spread it onto warm bread and enjoy!

*Enjoy Pumpkin Treats

Pumpkin is so wonderful; it's a shame most of us use it only in October and November. Here are some easy yet delicious recipes you might try all year:

PUMPKIN BREAD:

1⅓ cups vegetable oil

5 eggs

2 cups (16 oz. can) pumpkin purée

2 cups all-purpose flour

2 cups sugar

1 tsp. salt

2 tsp. cinnamon

1 tsp. nutmeg

1 tsp. baking soda

2 small packages (3.2 oz.) instant vanilla pudding

1 cup chopped walnuts (optional)

Preheat oven to 350°F. Mix oil, eggs, and pumpkin. Sift together flour, sugar, salt, cinnamon, nutmeg, baking soda, and pudding packets. Mix well. Stir in the nuts. Pour into 2 greased loaf pans and bake at 350°F for 1 hour.

PUMPKIN BARS:

4 eggs

1⅔ cups sugar

1 cup vegetable oil

1 can (16 oz.) pumpkin purée

2 cups all-purpose flour

2 tsp. baking powder

2 tsp. cinnamon

1 tsp. salt

1 tsp. baking soda

FROSTING:

3 oz. softened cream cheese

½ cup softened butter

1 tsp. vanilla

2 cups confectioners' sugar

Preheat oven to 350°F. Beat together sugar, vegetable oil, and pumpkin purée. In a separate bowl, stir together flour, baking powder, cinnamon, salt, and baking soda. Combine with pumpkin mixture and spread in ungreased jelly-roll pan or a cookie sheet with sides. Bake for 25 to 30 minutes. Cool.

FROSTING:

Combine softened cream cheese, butter, vanilla, and powdered sugar. Frost bars. Makes 30 bars or more.

PUMPKIN CRISP:

1 can (29 oz.) pumpkin purée

1¼ cups sugar

2 tsp. cinnamon

½ tsp. ginger

1 tsp. nutmeg

1 can (13 oz.) evaporated milk

3 lightly beaten eggs

1 box (18.5–20 oz.) yellow cake mix

1 cup melted butter

Preheat oven to 350°F. Mix can of pumpkin purée with sugar, cinnamon, ginger, nutmeg, evaporated (not condensed) milk, and eggs. Pour into a greased 9 x 13 pan. Sprinkle cake mix on top, then drizzle the melted butter. Bake for 1 hour or until the topping is golden brown.

*Have an Invention Convention

Encourage your kids to be problem solvers and to come up with clever ideas and inventions. You might even have a yearly "Invention Convention" to display their latest technology.

*Design Your Own City

Go on an excursion around town to see how many different architectural designs you can find. Look for unusual cornices, domes, finials, and columns. Then go home and make your own miniature city.

Use a paper towel tube to make a tower and curl strips of paper to make Corinthian column tops. Make "stained glass" church windows with colored tissue paper ironed onto freezer paper. Cover clean, empty boxes with popsicle sticks or construction paper. Milk cartons have naturally vaulted roof lines, or could be topped with a pinwheel for a quick windmill. A mirror makes a fun ice skating rink. Surround your town with a train track made from toothpicks, or a road or castle wall made from Styrofoam packing "peanuts" (painted gray, they look like real rocks). Tiny twigs would make good trees. Dip ends in white glue, then in crumbled, dry leaves (or in bits of green yarn or confetti) to make the leaves. Toy animals can fill a farm or zoo.

Be sure to name your city for its founder. Anyone for Zacharyville, Jennyland, or Brandonberg? Add a clay statue of your child in a triumphant pose in Cassidy Square, or in front of Shawn Hall.

*Have Some Old-Fashioned Fun

Let kids learn about yesteryear and enjoy some of the ways families grew close in times gone by. Create an old-time radio show with sound effects. Cornstarch scrunched in your fist sounds like feet walking on snow. Jiggle aluminum foil to simulate lightning. Shake coins in an empty Band-Aid box to sound like a train. Don't forget to include old-time commercials.

Have an old-fashioned taffy pull (see pg. 42), shake whipping cream into butter (see pg. 77), or make lemonade from scratch. Make hollyhock dolls or carved apple dolls (see pg. 76). Sing around the piano (or a tape recorder), and try some harmonies. Keep a hula hoop rolling outdoors by running alongside it and hitting it with a stick.

HALLOWEEN

*Messages from the Good Witch

A friend of mine started this fun tradition. Each day in October, a special Good Witch leaves notes for her children in unusual places. Often they rhyme, and they always extol a virtue. Sometimes the witch tells a little poem about a bat, a vampire, a cat, or a ghoul who learned to share, tell the truth, etc. If your family reads the Bible, you could even find the solution to a problem posed by the witch in a specific verse of scripture. On Halloween, the Good Witch (just like Santa) actually shows up and tells a fun story to the children before leaving them treats and advising them to be good and always do what's right. This can be a cute way to make Halloween into a more substantial holiday than merely candy-gathering.

*Make Ghostly Candies

Halloween treats are a snap with this easy idea. Melt white chocolate chips in a double boiler over simmering water. Line a baking sheet with waxed paper. Now pour puddles of the melted chips onto the waxed paper, in ghostly shapes. Press dark chocolate chips into the ghosts for eyes. Insert sticks and let harden in the refrigerator.

*Make a Graveyard Cake

Bake a cake in a 9 x 13 pan. Frost the top green to resemble grass. Now frost some Fig Newtons or Pepperidge Farm cookies gray by mixing black cake tint into white frosting. Then press the cookies halfway into the cake to resemble headstones. Stick some of your candy ghosts into the scene!

*Drench the Candles

When it's time to blow out the candles inside your carved pumpkins, make it a game. Give each child a squirt gun (outside) and see who can shoot through the carved holes to put out her candle first.

*Make Remote Control Ghosts

Just drape a thin sheet of chiffon or cheese-cloth over a remote control car, hide it with the control box, then send your ghost reeling across the floor!

*Hunt for Hints

Sometimes safety and weather prohibit trick-or-treating. But you can still have fun by staging an indoor treat-hunt. Place clues throughout the house (rhyming clues are a fun touch), each leading to the next (and each one attached to a piece of candy).

When your child finds all the clues, there's a special treat awaiting—maybe a new toy or game!

*Make Tarantula Cupcakes

Whip up a batch of white cupcakes and tint the batter orange, using a concentrated cake coloring. Bake as directed. When cool, turn cupcakes upside down to form the spider bodies. Frost with black-tinted icing, then insert 6-inch segments of black shoelace licorice for legs. Press two red cinnamon candies into the icing for eyes. Yikes! Yum!

*If It's Raining Black Cats

Many areas of the country get rain or snow in October. Design a Halloween umbrella you can use all month, then again when it's time to trick-or-treat. Use fabric paints to adorn an umbrella with Halloween motifs: black cats, bats, candy corn, ghosts, pumpkins, witches. If you're using an umbrella when you trick-or-treat, make your designs with reflective stickers or glow-in-the-dark tape.

*Buckets of Candy

Let your kids make their own costumes. Our eldest, Richie, decided to be a trash can one year and found that, for less than five dollars, he could purchase a new, clean plastic garbage can and cut leg holes in the bottom. He hung it from his shoulders with rope. He was soon the biggest candy collector on the block! The lid was his hat.

Also, when Bob and I were pregnant with our son Cassidy, I pinned three black circles onto a black sweater and went as a bowling ball. Bob wore a hooded white sweatshirt and went as a pin. See how creative you can be.

*Make Your Own Soundtrack

Gather party guests around a microphone and make an audio recording of their best scary sounds. Have a prize for best cat meow, best squeaky door, best witch cackle, best shriek, best rattling chain, and of course, best "boo!" Then save the tape and play it for trick-or-treaters.

*Edible Masks

Let kids make masks using safety scissors and fruit leather. Start with a round Fruit Roll-up, cutting eye holes and a mouth. Now let them decorate the face with colorful hair, scars, warts, eyebrows, fangs—you name it—using more fruit leather they can cut into smaller pieces and press on.

*Spider Web Bread

This easy treat is always a big hit. Purchase frozen bread dough or prepared cornbread sticks in chilled cans. If you're using bread, thaw one loaf and roll into "snakes." On a greased baking sheet or pizza pan, press lengths of dough into a spider web shape, draping the web between the "spokes" in a scalloped pattern. Bake at 350°F for 15 minutes, or until golden. Decorate with edible spiders if you like.

*Trunk or Treat

A great way to ensure your children's safety (and still let them gather lots of candy) is to gather with your school, church, or neighborhood and stage a "Trunk or Treat" event. Everyone parks their car so the tailgates form a circle around the church or school.

Kids then go from trunk to trunk, instead of from door to door, to gather treats. Decorate your cars with spider webs and jack-o'-lanterns, dress in costume, and hand out treats!

*A Seasonal Motto

Teach kids a trick-or-treat rule that says "If you don't glow, you don't go." Make sure all your kids wear reflective or glow-in-the-dark tape across their backs and chests, down their legs—whatever is necessary to make them visible to motorists. Remember to carry a flashlight and wear light clothing, too.

*Haunted House Luminaries

This is also a great way to recycle plastic milk jugs. Cut off the bottom, then cut out doors and windows (the open spout forms the chimney). Paint the "house" black with acrylic paint, then place it along your walkway over a short candle or bulb. Light will

seem to glow from the windows of your mansion. Makes a great night-light, too.

*Freeze Plastic Spiders in Ice Cubes

Then invite Aunt Edna over.

*Design a Spook Alley

Drape cobwebs through a darkened hallway, and be sure to have plenty of slimy noodles on hand. Kids love planning these even more than walking through them. Let their imaginations roam as they concoct spine-tingling ways to entertain their friends. Dry ice bubbling in a bowl of punch makes a fun ending to this chiller.

   *Put the ice in a bowl below the punch bowl so you won't risk anyone swallowing the dry ice.

*Make Orange Jacks

Draw a jack-o'-lantern face on oranges, or tangerines using a black grease pencil or indelible marker.

*Make Jell-O Jacks

Cut several oranges in half and hollow them out. Now fill the shell with orange Jell-O and chill until set. Slice into quarters and serve like orange sections. Orange sherbet makes a tasty alternative filling, too.

*Jack-O'-Lantern Spooks

Two to three weeks before Halloween, cut the top off an orange and scoop out the fruit. Using grease pencils or indelible markers, draw a jack-o'-lantern face on your orange. Now fill the empty orange rind with dirt and grass seed. Place in a sunny window and keep soil moist. Your spook will grow green hair that seems to be standing on end!

*Poppin' Jack

Make a giant popcorn cake that looks like a jack-o'-lantern.

1 package (16 oz.) marshmallows
½ cup butter (1 stick)
¼ cup vegetable oil
½ tsp. orange cake tint
16 cups popped popcorn

1 green gumdrop, for decorating

candy corn, for decorating

chocolate candies, for decorating

licorice (any color), for decorating

Melt marshmallows with butter, vegetable oil, and orange cake tint in a saucepan. Stir in popcorn, then press mixture firmly into two greased, same-size bowls. Remove half-spheres from bowls and press halves together to form a ball. Press on a green gumdrop for a stem, candy corn for teeth, chocolate candies for eyes, and lay the licorice flat for hair. Chill or let harden, then cut into slices and enjoy!

*Paint a Halloween Sweatshirt

You don't need to be an artist to create this easy shirt. Using fabric paint or acrylics, paint a couple of white ghosts on the front of a black sweatshirt. Be sure to leave holes for the eyes and mouth. Now paint candy corn around the neck to look like a neck-lace. Wear it all through October.

*Hide Candy Corn

Hide Halloween candy, Easter egg style, all around the house. Have a candy corn hunt!

*Serve Stew in a Pumpkin

Cut the top off a pumpkin and set the top aside. Scoop out the seeds. Brush the cavity with butter, then bake in a 9 x 13 pan at 350°F for 1 hour, or until pumpkin flesh is tender when pierced but still firm on the outside. Fill with your favorite hot stew, cover with the lid, and serve.

*Decorate Caramel Apples

Don't just stop with caramel—decorate it to look like a jack-o'-lantern. Or cover it com-pletely with M&Ms.

Another great idea is to make orange popcorn balls and press on a pumpkin face with dark brown M&Ms.

ORANGE POPCORN BALLS:

1 cup sugar

1 cup light corn syrup

1 package (6 oz.) orange gelatin

7–8 cups popcorn

Stir together sugar and light corn syrup in a small saucepan over high heat. Add orange gelatin powder. When mixture comes to a boil, remove from heat and pour over pop-corn. With buttered hand, form mixture into balls. Press candies onto the balls when they are almost cool.

*Spare Teeth

Instead of giving candy to trick-or-treaters, give out stickers, small toys, Pogs, collector cards, or coins.

*Play "Stick the Wart on the Witches Nose"

It's a great alternative to "Pin the Tail on the Donkey."

*Make a Giant Spider

Fill a black trash bag with autumn leaves or rumpled newspaper. This will form the spider's body. Now cut another trash bag into strips and attach these for the legs. Paint a scary face on your spider and display it on your porch.

*Have Jack-O'-Lanterns for Breakfast

Try two tasty ideas:

1. Cover an English muffin with grated cheese (moisten with mayonnaise), then use pieces of black olives for eyes, nose, and mouth.

2. Spread a bagel with orange-tinted cream cheese. Use raisins for the eyes, nose, and mouth.

*Make Ghosts

Dip a 2-foot square of cheesecloth into white liquid starch. Place a tennis ball atop an empty soda bottle, then cover with the wet cheesecloth. If you want your ghost to have arms, place a bent hanger under the ball before you top it with the cheesecloth. Place your ghost on waxed paper to dry, then remove the bottle, hanger, and ball. Your transparent ghost will keep its shape and make a magical decoration. Draw eyes and a mouth if you wish.

FOR THE PARENTS

*Make Car Pooling Safe

If you have a tot who's reluctant to wear a seat belt, try this trick. Tell them it's actually a Power Belt. Inject some action-hero excitement into the game and pretend you're in a space ship. Lock on your invisible helmets. Put on your laser gloves. Power up!

*Rewrite the Endings

Often kids are troubled by movies and stories we think look pretty harmless. Even standard fairy tales can be upsetting to a sensitive child (and usually you discover their fears right at bedtime). We've made a game of "rewriting" the endings to make them happier or more acceptable. We let the child say what he wished would have happened, or how he could have improved the outcome. Often, he improves upon the story! And it certainly helps him feel better about whatever upset him.

*Display Your Kids' Art

Watch your kids swell with pride when their efforts are hung in your home. Hang them on the refrigerator with a magnet, or establish a special bulletin board just for artwork. We like to slide their paintings under a piece of clear plastic on the dining table. It protects them from spills while showcasing them for all of us to admire over dinner. We also use the plastic to showcase maps, charts, and other educational materials the kids can look at while they're eating.

*Make Lunch Box Surprises

It only takes a few seconds to write a quick love note on a napkin or apply a sticker. We like to write a riddle and see if our children can figure it out before they get home.

*Organize Winter Entrances

Establish bins for homework and backpacks so kids' notes and assignments don't get lost. If you have space, consider installing metal lockers near the back door so kids can put away wet boots and coats instead of dumping them in the all-too-familiar pile.

*Give Kids Three "Booster Shots" to Bring Up Their Grades

Think like a teacher. Teach kids to:

1. Double check all their work.

2. Look in the index of textbooks—test questions often come from the glossary and index.

3. Make up their own test questions.

*Have Dates with Your Kids

Sometimes school and extracurricular activities seem to fill our children's lives, and before you know it, they're going off to college. Make time to plan dates with your kids—moments when it's just the two of you having fun together. At least once a month, spend a few hours with your child doing something he enjoys. Let him have a break from being "the oldest" or "the youngest." Let him just be an individual you love.

*Tough Choices

The start of school is a good time to review family ethics and honesty. Ask your child to play a game called "What If" and see what he would do in certain situations. What if you spilled paint and the teacher blamed another child for it? What if a boy accidentally put his toy in your backpack, thinking it was his? What if the clerk gives you back too much change? What if the teacher lost the tests and asked each child to report the score they had gotten? What if you saw the answers to a teacher's quiz during recess? What if a book club mailed you more books than you paid for? What if your friend wants you to give her the answer during a test? You might tell your child that integrity is doing the right thing, even if you knew you would never be found out.

*Send 'Em Off in Style

For families whose children are leaving for college, here are some great gifts to help them make the transition:

1. A personalized laundry bag filled with

packets of detergent and a roll of quarters.

2. Stamped, addressed envelopes so they'll be sure to write.

3. Your ten easiest recipes.

4. A telephone calling card worth several calls home.

5. A fix-it kit containing nails, a hammer, a screwdriver, tape, scissors, a tape measure, pliers, and first aid items.

6. A cassette recording of everyone in the family telling your child how much they are loved. Don't forget to enclose photos.

7. A box of their favorite cookies, or a cookie-of-the-month club you make yourself.

8. A list of important information—medical insurance numbers, bank account numbers, doctor and dentist phone numbers, eyeglass prescriptions, copies of important receipts and warranties, etc.

9. A travel-size alarm clock.

10. A pillowcase signed by everyone in the family in washable fabric ink. You can even write notes of encouragement on it.

11. A new subscription to a magazine about their college major or something else they enjoy.

12. A camera and film so they can send home pictures of their new surroundings.

*Warm Up with a One-Minute Hug

Hug someone in your family for sixty seconds. You'll be amazed at the closeness you'll feel after the giggles die down. You'll melt away stress knots, even open doors to intimacy and communication that can increase family solidarity and love.

*Vote

November is voting month. Talk about what this means and how it works. You might create a family ballot to vote for some fun things: best bedtime story, favorite restaurant, best zoo animal, and so on. Tally the votes and teach the meaning of majority rule: If the majority votes for chocolate cake, chocolate cake it is. (But those who voted for ice cream may demand a recount!)

*Whip Up Indoor Snow Sculptures

This is a real favorite. In a mixing bowl, beat soap flakes (Ivory detergent is best) with a few drops of water. When the lather gets stiff, let your kids sculpt with it on a cookie sheet. They can create snow men, igloos, handprints—whatever they want. And, unlike working with clay, when they're finished, your kids' hands are guaranteed to be clean!

*Warm Up Teddy

Toss your child's favorite stuffed animal into the dryer just before he goes to bed. Let it fluff for a few minutes, just enough to get nice and warm. When your little one snuggles down under the covers tonight, he'll hold a toasty warm cuddly in his arms.

*Draw with Your Toes

Hold a pen or crayon between your toes, then draw or write on a piece of paper. Are you right- or left-footed? If this doesn't get you giggling, nothing will.

*Make Banks

Start the new year off right by learning to save money. Our kids have shoeboxes divided into compartments, with four slits cut into the lids. Each slit is for a different kind of saving: college, spending, etc. Another idea is to cover an empty can with papier-mâché (see pg. 45), rest it on four corks (with a fifth cork for the nose), and make a piggy bank. A snap-on plastic lid can be cut for the coin slit. Wrap a pipe cleaner around a pencil to make it curly enough for a tail.

*Put Together a Family Time Capsule

This is also a terrific idea for family reunions. Everyone contributes one (or five) items that depict life—or your family—in this year. Put all the objects into a box or can and seal it until . . . (you pick the year for opening).

*Make Silhouettes of Your Child's Profile

In a darkened room, shine one lamp brightly on a wall. Tape a large sheet of white paper to the wall and place your child on a chair between the paper and the light. You may need to experiment with the lamp placement to produce a sharp shadow line. Lightly trace your child's silhouette in pencil.

Most kids have a hard time sitting still, so bring extra patience to this project.

After you've sketched the profile, use it as a pattern to cut out another version, this time on heavier, black paper. Next mount the black silhouette on a larger sheet of white poster-board, which you then may frame (don't forget to cut out copies for relatives). Our kids also made a handprint in paint, below their silhouette.

Before you turn off the lamp, put on a puppet show, forming animals with your hands.

*Invent New Exercises

Don't let inclement weather keep you from staying in shape. Let your kids get creative and come up with new exercises to try. Videotape them if you wish—maybe your children could even make an exercise video to music.

*Draw Pennies

Celebrate Abraham Lincoln's birthday by sketching pennies. As the kids draw, point out the tiny image of Lincoln in the impression of the Memorial on the back of the penny. Tell them the legend of Lincoln's extraordinary honesty: One day when he was working as a clerk in a store, a woman over-paid by one cent. Lincoln chased after her for a long way, just to return the penny. You can also tell kids about his other achievements, like his role in abolishing slavery in the United States. Older kids can try to sketch an exact replica of a penny from memory.

Another interesting use for a penny is for checking the wear on your tires. Insert a penny, head first, into the groove of a tire. If all of Lincoln's head shows, your tires are getting bald and need replacing.

*Shine Pennies

This is so magical and fun, kids will ask to do it again and again. Dip some pennies into ketchup and let them set for just a minute. Now wipe the pennies clean and voilà! They'll shine. (Taco sauce or any acidic tomato sauce will shine copper, too. Or try a solution of one-half cup vinegar and four tablespoons of salt.)

*Warm Chilly Toes

Here's a great way to warm your tootsies! Simply pour a two-pound bag of uncooked white rice into a clean tube sock. Tie it in a knot, then microwave on full power for two minutes. This heating pad will stay warm for a long time, and will easily form around a sore neck, or cold feet. Decorate the sock with a face and ears to make a teddy bear or a mouse.

*Freeze a Miniature Snowman

Find a place in your freezer and tuck away a smaller version of the one in your yard. Just stack three snowballs together. What a fun centerpiece for a summer birthday party!

*Make a Family Flag

This wonderful project can be drawn on a poster, sewn from fabric, or glued with felt. Let each member of the family contribute ideas, colors, and symbols that depict your values. Your flag can be a rectangle, a shield, a banner, or a heart. You can divide it into quadrants, use a family crest, or splash it with family handprints. You can attach streamers bearing each child's name or a motto you believe in, such as "United We Stand," "Learn, Love, & Lead," "Do Your Best," "Return with Honor," etc. Hang your flag on a door, over the mantle, on a prominent wall, in kids' bedrooms, or from a flagpole outside. Reproduce your design on T-shirts: It's great for reunions, camping tents, stationery, stickers, and book covers.

*Celebrate the First Snow

Establish a tradition, such as popping corn or making homemade chili, that always announces the beginning of winter. Maybe you can rent a favorite movie or make a cake. Let it be something your kids look forward to every year.

*Make a Wreath

Here's a fun way to dry kids' snowy mittens and hats. Simply hang S-hooks on a three-dollar grapevine wreath from the craft store; use four hooks per child. Then hang the wreath in your "mud room," where the kids come in wet from playing in the snow. Let them hang their mittens, hats, and scarves on the wreath. It's colorful, functional, and there are no more sopping clothes on the floor!

*Make Snow Cream

If you live where it snows, make snow cream. Scoop up a bowl of fresh, clean snow (just under the top layer is cleanest), and mix it with heated maple syrup and cream. Adjust amounts to your taste. Or, stir the snow with fruit juice. Add food coloring if you wish.

*Have a Snow-Sculpting Contest

Invite the neighbors and fill your lawn with objects of art. You can even get fancy and paint them. Be sure to serve hot cocoa and give each sculpture an award (most unusual, most wintry, most comical, etc.)

*Have Some Quiet Fun

Like it or not, there are certain times when children have to know how to entertain themselves quietly—in churches, in hospitals, in airplanes, and in office meetings. Here are twelve guaranteed noise-busters you can pack along to insure tranquillity:

1. Knot Now. See how many knots your child can tie in a length of string. Then undo them and see if you can tie even more. Older kids can time themselves to see how fast they can untie knots. A length of string can also be used to string beads, pasta, or Cheerios. Or, dangle the string on carpet to make a picture. To erase, just pull on the string! Strings can also be used to practice braiding, weaving, macrame, or shoe-tying.

2. Clay Play. Bring the kind that won't dry out and crumble. Then, instead of making the trip a zoo, your kid can spend quiet time sculpting one.

3. Puzzlemania. Use old Christmas cards, postcards, even extra school photos to make jig-saw puzzles that can go anywhere. Older kids can assemble puzzles with many parts, while toddlers will enjoy piecing together a picture of only three or four sections. Store each mini-puzzle in its own protective envelope.

4. Stick 'Em Up. Bring along an envelope containing paper and as many stickers as you can round up. Stars, dots, even old address labels or colored tape can be used to create art quietly.

5. Old Favorites. Kids can occupy themselves for hours with just pencils and paper. Teach them Hangman, Tic Tac Toe, and to connect dots on a grid to make the most enclosed boxes. If there's no one to play with, kids can create their own mazes, miniature board games, crossword puzzles, and dot-to-dot pictures.

6. Twist But Don't Shout. Twist ties that come with plastic bags have saved our sanity in many a church meeting. Kids can fashion these quiet building tools into endless designs, even jewelry and eyeglasses.

7. Origami. Learn the basics of a few simple folding techniques and your kids can entertain themselves for hours without making a peep. Instead, they'll make cranes, frogs, lions, and grand pianos! Origami is a nifty challenge for children of any age, even a young one who is learning to make a

simple boat. The only thing you'll need are sheets of square paper.

8. Clock Watch. This is a good guessing game that really makes time fly. The only thing you need is a wristwatch or clock with a second hand. Have your child close her eyes and open them when she thinks ten seconds are up. Was she early? Late? Now try thirty seconds or a full minute. Try again, and again!

9. Book 'Em!. Purchase a couple of inexpensive books to bring out as a surprise. Even children too young to read will enjoy looking at a new book. Older kids will be delighted that you brought along a paperback by their favorite author.

10. That Felt Great! For just pennies you can buy hours of entertainment. Purchase a few squares of colored felt. Leave one square uncut for a "flannel board," then cut the others into any shapes you like. Your child can make geometric designs, landscapes, and stories just by arranging the pieces of felt on the larger one and taking them off again. Slip it all into a resealable plastic bag, and you have a traveling show that won't make a sound.

11. Video Games. This is finally the time and place for them. Just make sure the sound is turned completely off, and it's a great way to insure silence. You're not letting your kids' minds rot—this is an unusual situation that requires a child to be quietly occupied. You aren't letting the games take the place of quality family time. How much quality time can you offer in the middle of a meeting, anyway?

Video games aren't for outings where you want kids to pay attention, but they're perfect for grown-up places where children occasionally wind up, like the rare office meeting when you simply had to bring them with you.

12. Sock It to 'Em. Finally, there's a use for all those stray socks that the washing machine didn't eat. Draw faces on them and make hand puppets. Get creative, and glue on some yarn hair or a bow tie. Just make sure the stars of the show keep their voices down.

THANKSGIVING

*Make Autumn Place Mats

Gather beautiful fall leaves, then glue them to bright paper. Cover with laminating plastic.

*Make Pine-Cone Turkey Place Cards

Turn a pine cone on its side to form the turkey's body. From construction paper, cut a turkey's head and feathers. Glue the neck to the small end of the cone and fan out the feathers to glue to the wide end. Write each guest's name on the tail feathers.

*Express Gratitude

During your feast, go around the table and let each person share something they're thankful for.

*Trace Turkeys

Trace your child's hand, then help her turn the tracing into a turkey. Color the thumb like a turkey's head, while the fingers become colorful feathers.

*Make Rain Sticks

You can duplicate the wonderful instruments inspired by Native American rain sticks. Press toothpicks at random points through the sides of an empty wrapping paper tube. Now cover one end of the tube with paper and secure with tape or rubber bands. Insert dried beans, rice, or small pebbles. Cover the other end the same way. Tip your rain stick to hear the sound it makes as the pebbles bounce against the toothpicks.

*Create "Straw" Wreaths

Make wreaths by mixing crumbled Shredded Wheat with enough white craft glue to moisten it. Shape the mixture into a circle on a sheet of waxed paper and let dry. Add a raffia bow and some pine cones, if you wish.

*Spell It

Give children a sheet of paper with the word "Thanksgiving" written vertically down the left side. Let them list things they are

thankful for which start with each letter in the word "Thanksgiving."

*Remember the Wildlife

Our kids look forward to this activity as much as they do to our Thanksgiving feast. We always take bags of nuts and birdseed and scatter it outside for the squirrels and birds.

*Pop Up Some Fun

Remind everyone that the Native Americans showed the European settlers how to grow corn. Here are five great ways to celebrate this fun food:

1. Grow your own popcorn. Fill a glass jar with damp paper towels. Press unpopped popcorn kernels between the towels and place it in a sunny window. Keep it damp, and in a few days your popcorn will sprout.

2. Make a popcorn wreath. Cover a small circle of Styrofoam with white craft glue. Now dip it into a bowl of unpopped kernels, scooping them onto the glue—completely covering it. Let dry on a paper towel. Add a bow, and you have a golden harvest wreath.

3. Make a popcorn cake.

1 (16 oz.) package of marshmallows
½ cup butter (1 stick)
¼ cup vegetable oil
16 cups of popped popcorn
1 cup of M&Ms

Melt package of marshmallows with butter and vegetable oil in a saucepan. Place popcorn in a large bowl, then stir in marshmallow mixture. Add M&Ms. Spread popcorn mixture firmly into a greased 10-inch Bundt pan; chill. Unmold onto serving plate and slice. This also makes a fun gift.

4. Next time you pop up some popcorn, play this game: Be first to clap when you hear the first kernel pop. Win the first taste!

5. Be the world's most famous popcorn sculptor! Use the popcorn cake recipe, but instead of pressing it into a pan, shape it into whatever you wish. Spray hands with non-stick coating, then sculpt a snowman, an igloo, maybe even a bust of someone in the family! Or, just make popcorn balls. Beware: Art work may be eaten when you're not looking!

*Make a Miniature Thanksgiving Cornucopia

Use a sugar cone for the "horn of plenty" and tiny foods or candies for the bounty that flows from it. Your harvest can include raisins, peas, berries, grapes, cereal, tiny fruit snacks, marzipan, and other small edibles. This makes a pretty centerpiece, too.

*Bake a Bread Cornucopia

We love to adorn our Thanksgiving table with this spectacular centerpiece. Wrap bread dough (homemade or store-bought) around a cone of aluminum foil and brush it with egg yolk to make it shiny. Bake until crispy golden, then cool. Remove the aluminum cone, and fill the cornucopia with delicious fruits. For extra elegance, give the fruit a frosty coating: Dip fruit in egg whites, then sugar, then let dry on waxed paper. Grapes, persimmons, apples, lemons—everything sparkles with its crystal coating. ***Coated fruit should not be eaten!**

CHANUKAH

*Spin a Dreidl

Cut one of the sections from a cardboard egg carton. Draw one of each of the Hebrew letters—Nun, Gimel, Hay, and Shin—on the four sides of the section. Push a sharpened pencil into and through the bottom, leaving the blunt or eraser end

| Shin | Hey | Gimel | Nun |

extended for twirling. Cut out and glue a flat cover made of paper for the open end. Now your top is ready to spin!

*Make a Star of David

Draw a six-pointed star with white glue on a sheet of waxed paper. You may want to place a pattern under the waxed paper for your child to follow. *Please note: don't fill it in with glue; just leave it as an outline. Now sprinkle the star with silver or blue glitter. When it's dry, peel off the waxed paper and hang it in a window!

*Make a Chanukah Gift

Here's an easy project for little ones to craft: Place blue and white marbles or beads in the lid of a jar. Arrange them in the shape of a Star of David. Now squirt white glue into the lid, so that the marbles are sitting in a shallow puddle of glue. In a day or two, the glue will harden and become clear. If you like, glue fancy trim or braiding around the jar lid.

*Make Your Own Gilded Chocolate Coins

Simply melt your favorite chocolate chips in the microwave or in the top of a double boiler, and let droplets harden on waxed paper. As they cool, press a coin against them to imprint its face. When completely cool, wrap the candies in gold or silver-colored foil and present them in a drawstring pouch.

*Make a Menorah

Make eight easy candles for the holiday. Ahead of time, collect eight empty baby food jars, or use eight 8-ounce jam jars. Let Mom or Dad melt paraffin wax (available in grocery stores) in aluminum pie tins over low heat. Add peeled blue or silver crayons for color. Place a candle wick in each jar, then pour in wax and let harden. Line up the jars, then light a different one each night of Chanukah. Try different sized jars and different shades of colored wax for each candle.

CHRISTMAS

*Family Calendar

This one makes a knock-out gift for grandparents. You can dig back through the year for priceless seasonal photo negatives, or stage it using just one roll of film. Depict all the holidays, dragging out the Halloween costumes, the Easter baskets, cutting paper hearts, etc. Dress your kids and give them props to go with every month. Develop your roll of film. Now create a twelve-month calendar by drawing the boxes for the days (or use a purchased calendar), and paste the appropriate family snapshot on each page. Bind together, and you're all set.

*"Twelve Days of Christmas" for Another Family

This will be one Christmas your kids never forget. They might even ask to do it for someone new each year. Choose a family to surprise, then anonymously deliver twelve gifts to them, one each day before Christmas (I know, I know—the actual twelve days of Christmas do not fall on these actual dates. But this way is more fun.) Write a little clue or poem to go with each delivery, if you wish. This is a great way to excite children about the joy of giving.

DAY ONE: A pretty box of pears, from the tree the partridge sat in.

DAY TWO: Two bars of Dove soap (the turtle doves got away clean!). Or, two chocolate-pecan turtle candies.

DAY THREE: One fresh whole chicken. Or, frozen game hens, or a trio of French cheeses wrapped in a chicken-printed napkin.

DAY FOUR: A toy phone so you can answer the calling birds.

DAY FIVE: Five donuts, bagels, or other ring-shaped treats.

DAY SIX: Fresh eggs from the six geese a-laying.

DAY SEVEN: Seven fronds-a-swimming (seven sprigs of palm or fern in a vase of water).

DAY EIGHT: Milk the maids brought in. (Fill a rubber glove with water, and tie it to a gallon of milk).

DAY NINE: A recording of music that nine ladies might dance to (a tape of Christmas music—the older and funnier the better).

DAY TEN: A jump rope for leaping into the New Year.

DAY ELEVEN: An eleven-dollar gift certificate for their next plumbing bill, to fix pipes.

DAY TWELVE: An empty box or tin, shaped and decorated like a drum and filled with goodies from the drummers. Use candy canes for drum sticks.

On the last day, you can reveal yourselves with a special goodie or Christmas gift. Be sure to carol when you arrive, perhaps singing "The Twelve Days of Christmas."

*Use Twinkle Lights for a Night Light

Let kids use a cluster of twinkle lights for a night light this month. If you want to get elaborate—like my son Brandon—make a Sears Tower replica from papier-mâché (see pg. 45), drill holes for the window lights, then stuff a strand of twinkle lights inside. His window looked like a city skyline!

*Help Kids Surprise Their Siblings

Christmas is the ideal time to be an elf, doing secret good deeds. Help a youngster make his sister's bed for her, then tie the pillow with a ribbon. What other fun surprises can you plan?

*Make Post-it Guesses

For kids who have a hard time waiting to open presents under the tree, have them ease their suspense by writing or drawing their guesses on Post-It notes and attach them to the gifts. On Christmas morning, they can see if they guessed right!

*Make Trophies for Each Other

Have a plaque or trophy engraved for an off-beat accomplishment. My husband rewarded me for winning a beef cook-off by presenting me with a trophy that has a gold steer on top! One time some friends gave him a plaque with a bent toy car on it, to congratulate him for stunt driving (after he accidentally rolled a car over three times down a hill).

*It's a Wrap

There are so many clever ways to wrap gifts. Here are a few:

1. Explore nature for wonderful gift-wraps. One of the prettiest ways to wrap a candle, bottle, or jar of jam is to wrap it with a piece of birch bark and tie it with raffia. Add a dab of sealing wax for a truly elegant touch. Or, glue bay leaves to a box, then tie it with

gold cord. Magnolia leaves are another gorgeous covering. You can even give standard wrapping a beautiful touch by hot-gluing a sprig of pine or holly near the bow. Gift tags can be broad leaves, such as the magnolia, with names written on them in gold ink.

2. Fill a plastic bucket with summer-time gifts (sunglasses, beach towel, shovel, lotion, radio, thongs, etc.)

3. Inexpensive clay pots make great containers. Paint them first for a double gift.

4. Tie a pretty scarf around a box, and you've got wrapping that recycles. Even fabric remnants are often less expensive than wrapping paper, and the recipient can then use the fabric.

5. Inexpensive straw or cowboy hats (a dollar or two) have the perfect compartment to hold small gifts. They're especially good for holding accessories or garden gloves. To keep the gift inside its container, just cover the hat with colored cellophane, or tie the gift inside a bandanna and place it inside the hat.

6. Old books (twenty-five cents at a thrift shop or tag sale) can become marvelous secret compartments. Cut a hole through all the pages. You now have a safe for valuables, but you also have a clever gift box. Just put a small gift in the hole and tie the book closed with a ribbon.

7. Crocheted doilies (fifty cents at a thrift shop or tag sale), can be dipped in liquid starch and formed into muffin tins to make little cups. Fill with some straw or confetti and your gift, then wrap in transparent plastic or cellophane.

8. Lunch boxes make neat containers. Even new ones are cheap, but used ones can be found for just pennies. Cover with stickers and fill with a gift. Art supplies are a good idea.

9. Wrap gifts with newspaper comics, road maps, aluminum foil, or hand-stamped butcher paper.

10. Ornaments that open up with hollow insides (fifty cents at a craft shop) make superb containers for small gifts. Wrap your present in hay, tinsel, or tissue paper, and enclose it in an ornament. Decorate with paint, indelible markers, or stickers.

11. Use new pizza boxes. Available at pizza take-out restaurants, these are very inexpensive, and you can stencil an angel or paint a winter scene on them if you like.

12. Sponge-paint a brown paper lunch sack or cover it with stickers. Punch two holes on each side, an inch from the top edges, and tie with string.

13. Inexpensive pillowcases make super wraps, especially for gifts such as pajamas. Just tie a string around them to hold the gift inside, and you're set. Later, the recipient can sleep on your clever wrapper!

14. Homemade drawstring bags make it easy to wrap odd-shaped gifts. Just sew or hot-glue a rectangular pocket and thread a string through the hem.

*Give Gifts from the Kitchen

Bake a spice cake in a mason jar. Here's how:

2⅔ cups sugar

⅔ cup vegetable shortening

2 cups applesauce

4 eggs

⅔ cup water

3⅓ cups flour

2 tsp. baking soda

1 tsp. salt

1 tsp. cinnamon

2 tsp. cloves

½ tsp. baking powder

1 cup nuts or raisins (optional)

Preheat oven to 325°F. Mix sugar with shortening. Add applesauce, eggs, and water. Mix well until smooth. Add flour, baking soda, salt, cinnamon, cloves, baking powder, and mix well. Add a cup of nuts or raisins, if desired. Spray wide-mouthed pint jars with non-stick coating, and fill half full with batter. Bake for 45 minutes or until a toothpick inserted in center comes out clean. While cakes are still hot, screw on jar lids. Cover lid with a round of Christmas fabric and a pretty bow.

*Make a Snowman Kit

If you live where it snows, fill a box with all the trimmings for a snowman. This is a wonderful way to welcome a new neighbor. Pack up a carrot for the nose, two lumps of coal for the eyes, two sticks for the arms, big buttons, an old hat, and a scarf.

*Coat Spoons with Melted Chocolate

Melt chocolate chips of varying colors separately in the top of a double boiler over simmering water. Dip in spoons, then let them harden on waxed paper. Tie like a bouquet. They're great for stirring hot chocolate!

*Choose a Gift-Giving Theme

Themes can invigorate tired sock-and-tie gift lists. They can be fun, fanciful, or practical. When everyone agrees on a theme, your shopping becomes more focused and making up your gift list becomes a snap. Whether your budget is little or lavish, one of these fifteen themes might be a good fit for your family:

1. The Great Outdoors. Camping equipment, lawn furniture, luggage, outdoor sporting goods, jackets, a hammock, a camera, even houseplants to create an outdoors effect.

2. Happy Meals. How about filling your kitchen with culinary gadgets, cookbooks, and a coupon for a date to your favorite restaurant?

3. The Universal Language. A wife selected this theme, thinking it was common knowledge that music is the universal language. She purchased a music box, a CD player, and some tickets to a concert. Her husband, however, sheepishly admitted that he thought love was the universal language, and blushed as his wife opened her gifts: negligees, scented oils, and books on sprucing up one's love life.

4. No Place Like Home. Perfect for household items and decorating accents.

5. Back to the Future. These are items you don't need today, but might soon: An investment guide for the future entrepreneur; support hose and a rocking chair; a baseball mitt for the new baby; a trophy for a beginning athlete; bonbons for the overworked; earplugs for the soon-to-be parents; or the latest fashions or state-of-the-art equipment.

6. Are You Game? Athletic gear, tickets to an amusement park or ball game, puzzles, board games, video game software, even coupons for daring adventures like white-water rafting or hot air balloon rides.

7. Let It Snow: Ski equipment, sweaters, parkas, sleds, hot cocoa mugs, blankets, mittens, marshmallows for roasting, or bubbles for a hot bath.

8. Under the Sea. A pirate's chest of jewels, snorkeling equipment, an underwater camera, swimwear, coral jewelry, a boat ride, beach towels, an aquarium of fish, a beach umbrella, fishing tackle, or clam chowder.

9. The Wild West. Antiques, homemade chili, Western novels, horse-riding lessons, something gold, old-fashioned candy, a pocket watch, or Western wear. How about some red long underwear?

10. Handmade Only. All the gifts must be handmade—crafts, poems, artwork, goodies from the kitchen, woodworking, and sewing.

11. Only in the Movies: Microwave popcorn, cinema sound tracks, a director's chair, books and mugs featuring favorite characters, or costumes.

12. Around the World. A Chinese fan or puzzle, French perfume, Swiss chocolate, imported cheeses, Italian shoes, a stuffed koala, or tickets to an exciting destination.

13. Thanks for the Memories. Repair old photos of ancestors, give cameras or recording equipment, make scrapbooks, write a poem about wonderful past events, put slides on videotape, make a collection of favorite songs, or refurbish cherished items.

14. Pleasant Dreams. This one could range from pajamas and bedding to the fulfillment of personal dreams—if your husband has always wanted to swim with dolphins, pick a date and make arrangements. If your daughter has always wanted a china doll, give her the doll of her dreams.

15. Animal Crackers. Pets and supplies, books about animals, binoculars, bird feeders, bunny slippers, sheepskin car seat covers, an animal cookie jar, a leopard-print scarf, a butterfly kite, an ostrich egg, a crock of bee's honey, even "the cat's pajamas."

*Make Chocolate Nog

Mix equal parts hot chocolate and eggnog. It's like drinking a cream-filled chocolate truffle. You definitely gotta try this!

*Make a Candy Cane Pot

Glue candy canes around a flower pot or a can, then fill with a houseplant. Great gift for the schoolteacher.

*Make Cinnamon Candles

Glue cinnamon sticks of varying lengths all around a chunky candle. Tie with a ribbon, then light the candle and enjoy the cinnamon fragrance.

*Make a Tumbleweed Snowman

If you live in a hot, dry climate, stack three big tumbleweeds together to make a Southwestern cowboy snowman. Be sure to spray-paint them white!

*Use Christmas Flavors

Stir cinnamon and sugar or bits of candy cane into pancake batter. While you're at it, try new flavors to jazz up seasonal drinks—stir your hot cider with a cinnamon stick or your hot chocolate with a peppermint candy cane.

*Dip Pretzels in Chocolate

Get fancy: dip half in white, half in brown, then coat with nuts. Experiment with colored melting disks available at candy supply or craft stores.

*Send a Photo Christmas Card

There are lots of ways to make your photo extra special. Here are a baker's dozen:

1. Send stocking-shaped cards made from construction paper and have your family's faces pop out of the top.

2. Put mousse in everybody's hair so it stands straight up, then hold a string of Christmas lights so that it looks as though you're all getting electrocuted.

3. Let the baby of the family pop out of a giant, wrapped box as the other members of the family pretend to be opening a surprise.

4. Turn a sled over in the snow and have everyone pose around it as if they've just crashed and piled out in the snow.

5. Do an artsy close-up of your children's faces bedazzled by the glow of Christmas tree lights.

6. Dress like Santa Claus and pose one of the kids on his knee with a very long wish list. Have your Santa cringe as the rest of the family waits in line with their lists.

7. Go for the opposite of cold and wintry—send a picture of the family at the beach or on a pool float sipping lemonade.

8. Use the traditional posed portrait idea, but have everyone wear Santa hats.

9. Line up the kids and have them hold a "Merry Christmas" banner.

10. Get a great shot of the kids trick-or-treating (or stage it by dragging out their Halloween costumes), then write on each card, "Oops—wrong holiday!"

11. If one of your kids is missing his front teeth, get a great close-up of his grin and write on each card, "All I want for Christmas are my two front teeth!"

12. Dress the kids up in costumes to portray the Nativity scene or Dickens-era carolers.

13. Get a candid shot of the kids in action—painting Christmas scenes on your windows or assembling a gingerbread house.

*Create Look-a-Like Dolls

There are a couple of ways to do this. The easiest is by making paper dolls. First, take pictures of your child posing (in the same position) in a swim suit and various outfits. Then, cut out her picture and glue it to a stiff board; or simply glue a photo of your child's face to existing paper dolls.

The second way involves making a simple cloth doll and transferring her photo to the fabric using a special chemical kit (available at craft stores). Add the right color yarn for hair and try to dress the doll in clothes similar to one of your kid's favorite outfits. It can become a real heirloom.

*Hang Holiday Shapes in the Window

Hang Christmas or Chanukah cookie cutters with bright ribbon.

*Make Cranberry Cream

Mix a 15-ounce can of whole cranberries into 8 ounces of softened cream cheese, then fill a pie shell with the mixture and chill. Or spread this glorious pink filling between waffles for a luscious Christmas dessert.

*Leave Carrots for the Reindeer

Paint "For Rudolph" on a wooden shoe and fill it with fresh carrots!

*Make Eggnog Pops

Just pour eggnog into a paper cup or popsicle form, insert a stick, and freeze. When frozen, peel away cup or remove from form.

*Remember Pets

Make a drawstring bag and fill it with milk bones or cat toys. Write "Santa's Doggie Bag" in glitter paint on one side.

*Make Candy and Lace Ornaments

Thread white candy canes through eyelet lace and hang them on the tree.

*Paint Your Windows

Mix a bit of detergent with tempera paints (for easy cleanup) and let the kids paint candy canes, holly, snowflakes, trees, and snowmen on the outside of your windows. No art degree necessary!

*Wrap Up in Ribbon

For just pennies you can brighten the holidays with ribbon. Try a few of these ideas:

1. Put away your bookends and tie books together with a ribbon and fluffy bow.

2. Weave a sparkly ribbon through a loose-knit sweater.

3. Tie shoes with Christmas ribbon. Add a bell for fun.

4. Tie a red bow around Fido's neck.

5. Tie a pretty ribbon around a picture on the wall.

6. Wrap banisters and poles with red and white ribbon, candy-cane style.

7. Tie plump red bows around throw pillows.

8. Tie bright bows around the necks of your family's teddy bears, then arrange them on a window seat, hearth, or in a cozy corner.

9. Tie festive ribbons around candlesticks and stemware.

10. Tie ribbons onto chair backs. Experiment with red, green, gold, silver, plaid—even cranberry or teal.

11. Adorn your Christmas tree with fluffy bows and streamers of ribbon.

12. Replace drapery tie-backs with holiday sashes and bows.

13. Tie ribbon bows on baskets.

14. Tie brass or metal bells onto doorknobs with festive ribbons.

15. Weave colorful ribbons into a checkerboard, then use them to make festive Christmas stockings.

16. Suspend a thick dowel from your mantle using ribbon. Now, instead of hanging your stockings from nails, slide their loops over the dowel and position in a row.

*Research Your Family Tree

This really gives kids a sense of belonging and makes them excited about their ancestors. Begin with yourself, then branch out to your parents, grandparents, and so on. Fill in their names and, if possible, birthdates and locations. You also can find a free service that will help you put together this exciting puzzle. Who knows—maybe you'll find a prince or a pirate in your tree!

*Make a Paper Chain

This is a fun way for kids to count the days until Christmas. Just alternate loops of red and green construction paper, one loop for every day in December. Write a surprise message on each strip it might be the directions for finding a cookie or a coupon for a kiss. Maybe it's a scripture about Christmas or a hint about one of their gifts. One strip could list the phone number of a relative to call and wish Merry Christmas. How about a recipe for a quick Christmas treat? Each day the kids get to take off another loop and see what it says.

*Take the Plunge

This is a whimsical gift—almost a gag gift, but great fun. Buy inexpensive toilet plungers and decorate them as follows:

1. Top one with a wooden head and red nose to resemble Rudolph.

2. Wrap one with alternating red and white tape to resemble a candy cane.

3. Cover one with gold glitter for the truly elegant bath.

Have fun with it and see how many variations you can imagine.

*Trim a Tree for the Birds

Plan an outdoor tree-trimming party for the birds. Invite each child to bring something birds would like to eat to hang on the tree. Pine cones or bagels rolled in peanut butter and birdseed work great. How about a string of dried cranberries or popcorn?

*Fry Stars

Place star-shaped metal cookie cutters in the frying pan and fry eggs in star shapes.

*Make an Advent Calendar

Purchase a yard of red felt and cover it with 25 green pockets (small squares of felt, hot-glued onto the yard of felt, calendar-style).

Write the numbers 1 through 25 on each pocket. In each pocket, place a tiny ornament or candy. Hang the calendar from a dowel. As each day arrives, kids get to find out what's inside the pockets. For storage, roll up the calendar and keep it in an empty wrapping paper tube.

*Make Gelatin Trees

Chill lime gelatin in cone-shape paper cups, then tear away cups to make Christmas tree shapes. Decorate with cream cheese.

*Drink Peppermint Orange Juice

Roll an orange between your hands until it's soft. Now cut an X into the orange and slide in a peppermint candy straw. Kids can sip their orange juice right from the orange.

*Make Antique Christmas Stockings

Use torn quilts that are now useless as bed coverings. Cut them into stocking shapes and sew up some festive "heirloom" Christmas stockings.

*Fashion a Quick Centerpiece

1. Fill a clear bowl with shiny ball ornaments and sprigs of pine.

   2. Fill a basket with polished apples, greenery, and baby's breath.

   3. Press cloves into the skins of oranges, then display them in a bowl.

   4. Arrange fresh fruit to resemble a Christmas tree, stacking them pyramid-style. Hold the pieces together with broken toothpicks. For extra elegance, first coat the fruit with egg whites, then dip into granulated sugar for a frosty effect.

   *Coated fruit should not be eaten!

   5. Hollow out apples and use as candleholders. Place a votive candle in each apple. Cut off bottoms of apples for stability.

   6. Set votive candles in a tray of rock salt, to resemble snow.

*Simmer the Smells of Christmas

No need to invest in pricey simmering products. Just sprinkle some cinnamon, nutmeg, cloves, apple chunks and/or orange peels into simmering water.

*Make Red Ice

Freeze cranberry-juice ice cubes to brighten up a glass of 7-Up.

*Wrap Pictures Like Presents

Then hang them back up on the wall.

*Make a Cinnamon Roll Tree

Stack baked cinnamon rolls of decreasing size to form a delicious Christmas tree. Drizzle lacy icing over all. Makes a great gift!

*Make Gift Tags from Old Christmas Cards

Cut the fronts off last year's cards, punch a hole in one corner, and make beautiful package tags.

*Display Christmas Cards

Line cards up on a mantel. Drape a ribbon through a doorway and hang them over it. Tie ribbons around a mirror, then slide the cards beneath the ribbon to hold them in place. Or tape them to the back of your front door.

*Dress Up Cloth Napkins

Add an elegant touch to solid red or green napkins by sponge-painting gold stars onto them.

*Make Your Own Crayons

Save broken crayons, then divide them by color. Peel. Melt them in an aluminum pie tin over low heat. Pour into candy molds or muffin tins. Try mixing color in swirls. When cool, pop them out, and you'll have great chunky crayons to give as gifts or use yourself.

*Remember the Less Fortunate

Don't let a Christmas go by when you don't wrap some toys for the needy or work in a soup kitchen. Deliver blankets to the homeless or become a literacy teacher at the local library. Select a family to surprise, then one evening leave a basket of goodies on their porch. Ring the bell and run!

Another great way to make Christmas "other-centered," is to put only presents that you are planning to give to a pre-selected family beneath the tree. Label them "Girl, 7" or "Boy, 12" to go with the anonymous family you'll be surprising (churches and community groups can supply this information). As the gifts accumulate, your children will think of these other people instead of what they are going to get. Deliver your gifts a few days before Christmas, then put your own presents for each other under the tree.

*Decorate Candles

This is one of the simplest activities, but makes lovely gifts. You can borrow books from the library on how to make candles (it's incredibly easy), but kids who are too young to handle hot wax can decorate purchased candles. Using a dab of soft wax, attach sequins, leaves, and pretty jewels. Embossed sealing wax is a pretty addition to store-bought candles. Craft stores also have kits of pliable sheets of colored wax that can be cut into shapes and pressed onto candles. Older kids could even carve a picture into a chunky candle.

*Make Hobby Wreaths

These are wonderful gifts. Fasten items that focus on a loved one's hobby to an inexpensive grapevine or straw wreath. You might tie on spools of thread and a tape measure, paintbrushes, garden seed packets and tools, cooking utensils, scrolls of music, miniature dollhouse furniture, rolls of film—whatever your hobbyist likes.

*Make a Snowman for the Birds and Squirrels

Use seeds, peanut butter, nuts, unsweetened cereal, frozen berries, apple slices, and orange sections to decorate your creation.

*Use Christmas Cookie Cutters for Napkin Rings

These make great table settings. Afterward, you guests can take them home as fun party favors.

*Make Snowflakes and Angels

Make paper snowflakes and paper doll angels with the children. Glue the flakes and angels onto construction paper and you can also create original Christmas cards.

*Write to Santa

We always mail Santa a photocopy of our kids' letters, keeping the originals in a photo album. Priceless!

*Blow Frozen Bubbles

Blow bubbles outside, just as you would with the standard soap-and-wand set. But do it when the temperature dips below zero, and the bubbles will freeze in mid-air. They'll float along, covered with crystals, and when they pop, you'll see a little puff of powder!

KWANZAA

*String a Kwanzaa Necklace

Kwanzaa is a seven-day cultural holiday that is celebrated by African Americans and others of African descent. It begins on December 26. Seven candles are lighted—one each night. They symbolize unity (*Umoja*), self-determination (*Kujichagulia*), collective work and responsibility (*Ujima*), cooperative economics (*Ujamma*), purpose (*Nia*), creativity (*Kuumba*), and faith (*Imani*). The next-to-last day is marked by a lavish feast, *Kwanzaa Karamu*. For the celebration, your child can paint macaroni shells the traditional colors of Black unity: red, green, gold, and black. Let them dry, then string them into a necklace.

*Fashion a Kwanzaa Hat

Use stiff paper or tag board to cut a three-inch-wide strip that will wrap around your child's head. Staple it into a circle that fits snugly. Now hold the circular strip over additional paper and trace the circle. Cut the circle out and glue or tape it to the circular strip to form the top of the hat. Let your child paint or color it red, green, and black to honor Kwanzaa colors.

*Make a Candle Holder

Using items of harvest, you can make a whimsical *Kinara*—the holder for your seven candles—that represents the principles of Kwanzaa. Hollow out various squashes, gourds, apples, and pumpkins, making sure each hole is just large enough to hold a candle. (You may want to cut off the bottoms of the veggies as well, so they'll sit flat.) Group them together in a pretty display and light a different candle (black, red, and green) each night.

*Make a Unity Cup

Simply put, this cup, also called the *Kikombe cha umoja*, is used for your whole family to pour or drink libations to the ancestors of your past, present, and future. There are two ways you could make this cup.

From a craft store, purchase wax strips (the ones used for decorating candles) in Kwanzaa colors. Wrap the strips around the outside of a glass or a paper cup to follow the cup's shape. You can even cut out designs from contrasting colors and press them on. Pinch the wax strips to seal any gaps where liquid could leak. Now remove the paper or glass cup, and you have a colorful, striped, waterproof glass.

Or you can use the recipe for clay on page 18 to make your family's cup, then decorate it.

*Plant Your Values

Let your child choose seven plant seeds that he feels best represent the seven Kwanzaa values. These can be vegetables, flowers, even grass. Plant each one in a separate little pot to keep on a windowsill and label each with a value. As he waters and tends the plants, your child will see them grow. By spring, the plants might be big enough to transplant into an outdoor garden, and by next year's Kwanzaa you'll be harvesting its fruits.

VALENTINE'S DAY

Fill a Heart-Shaped Candy Box with Gifts
This is especially appreciated by someone watching their calories. (Freeze the chocolates for later, or give them to someone with a high metabolism!) Now fill the little paper cups with your love's favorites. Some fun ideas are silk flowers, earrings, scented soaps, golf balls, dime-store toys, pearls of bath oil. Teens might like nail polish or lipsticks in creamy Valentine pinks and reds.

Cherries—or cherry tomatoes—are a fun change for a dieter who loves fruit and who loves red! When the box is heart-shaped, anything inside says, "I love you."

*Make a Wreath of Love

Make a wreath of paper hearts, each heart listing something you believe in: love, honesty, laughter, forgiveness, etc.

*Wish the World a Happy Valentine's Day

If you live where it snows, tramp a heart-shaped path into your front lawn. Sprinkle it with cherry Jell-O. As the sun melts the top layer of snow, your heart will turn a vivid red.

*Bake a Heart-Shaped Pizza or Cookie

Simply press the dough into a heart shape instead of a circle. Spell "I Love You" or "Be Mine" with the toppings of the pizza, or swirl it on the cookie with delicious frosting. (Use baking parchment under any extra-large cookie so it will slide off the baking sheet more easily.) Another option: Bake a large, round sugar cookie, but cover it with pink, red, and white candies in a heart shape.

*Make Chocolate Boxes

Break a chocolate bar into squares. Use cement frosting (see "Sugar Eggs" on pg. 30) to fasten the squares of chocolate into a cube with an open top. Tuck a plump strawberry or a chocolate kiss inside.

*Eat Heart-Smart Foods

You can even make a whole red-themed meal of it. Choose from red-leaf lettuce, red gelatin, beets, salsa, shrimp, lobster, red pepper strips, spaghetti, tomato soup, strawberry milk, raspberries, cherry pie, and applesauce tinted pink with red cinnamon candies.

*Be a Phantom Helper

Do secret good deeds for members of your family, and leave a phantom calling card: a paper heart that says, "I love you."

*Make a Cookie Bouquet

Insert wooden sticks into heart-shaped cookies before they bake, to form the stems.

*Wrap Homemade Jellies and Breads with Red Ribbon

Valentine-printed fabric or paper makes a great wrap for homemade expressions of love. Draw red hearts with a marker on clear cellophane. Then wrap that over pink tissue paper. Tie with a luscious ribbon.

*Bake a Cream Puff Heart

Cream puffs are much easier to make than they appear to be.

DOUGH:

1 cup boiling water

½ cup (1 stick) butter

1 cup all-purpose flour

¼ tsp. salt

4 eggs at room temperature

RASPBERRY MOUSSE:

1 pound (16 oz.) softened cream cheese

1 cup raspberry jam

8 oz. frozen whipped topping

GLAZE:

3 cups confectioners' sugar

1 tsp. vanilla

2 tsp. milk

PUFFS:

Preheat oven at 400°F. Melt butter in the boiling water. Quickly stir in flour and salt. Blend well, cooking over medium heat until mixture forms a smooth ball that doesn't separate. Remove from heat for 10 minutes. Add eggs, one at a time, beating vigorously after each. Use ¼ cup of batter for each puff. To make a heart, arrange dollops of dough on a greased baking sheet in the shape of a heart. Bake for 30–35 minutes, or until golden. Split puff and remove any soft dough inside.

MOUSSE:

In a separate bowl, beat softened cream cheese with raspberry jam. Stir in thawed whipped topping and blend until smooth. Then fill empty puff with mixture. For a different taste, try strawberry ice cream instead.

GLAZE:

To make glaze, simply mix powdered sugar with a few drops of vanilla and enough milk to make it pouring consistency. Add the milk just a few drops at a time, as you won't need much. And if you like, use Domino's pink powdered sugar, which comes in strawberry flavor. Finally, drizzle mousse-filled puff with pink or white glaze.

*Sew a Heart-Shaped Pocket on a Pillowcase, for Love Notes

You can sew a pink satin heart in the corner of an existing pillowcase, or make a new pillowcase from Valentine-printed fabric (it's so easy—just a rectangle). My three-year-old daughter loves checking her pocket for little love notes.

*Make Heart-Shaped Pancakes

Three dots of batter poured onto the griddle will do it (think of Mickey Mouse's head). Top with strawberry syrup and whipped cream. Add a little teacup of pink roses and baby's breath at each place setting for an unforgettable Valentine breakfast.

*Make Strawberry Dumplings

This is one of my award-winning creations. Place one strawberry on each of 8 won ton skins (you can purchase them pre-packaged from the supermarket and most Chinese markets). Moisten edges of another 8 skins and cover the strawberries, pressing to seal all edges and form dumplings. Fry in 3 tablespoons of vegetable oil in a small skillet over high heat, turning frequently (5 minutes or until skins brown). Drain dumplings, dust lightly with powdered sugar, and serve with whipped topping.

*Let Love Grow

Empty some wildflower seeds into a pretty jar. Tell your Valentine to toss them where they may and watch as evidence of your love "grows."

*Plant a Valentine Garden

Plant a giant heart-shaped flower garden for your love to see. Make all the flowers red, pink, or white.

*Give a Book of Love

Purchase an inexpensive blank book. Fill it with all the things you love about the recipient. Be specific and recall anecdotes you cherish.

*Write a Love Song or a Poem

Compose one yourself, or hire someone to serenade your love with an old favorite. How about framing the sheet music to the song that's "yours"?

*Make a Coupon Book

Give coupons to your valentine. Kids love to compile these. How about "Redeem for ten kisses," or "Good for one car wash"?

*Send Flowers to Your Kids

Kids love surprises, and when a delivery of fresh flowers arrives from the florist—with their name on it—Wow!

*Weave a Heart

Weave a pretty ribbon through a sweater—in the shape of a heart.

*Make Heart-Shaped Cakes

It's easy to make heart-shaped cakes and cupcakes. For a cake, bake one 8-inch-square cake and one round one. After they cool, cut the round one in half and attach the two halves to two adjacent sides of your square. Voilà! This makes a heart shape.

For cupcakes, place a marble between the cupcake paper and the muffin tin, forcing the batter into a heart shape.

*Leave Valentines

Tuck a valentine into someone's pillow for a goodnight surprise.

*Weave Placemats

Weave strips of red and white construction paper into cheery placemats.

*Make a Valentine Tree

Bring a small tree branch in, and hang paper hearts from each twig. On every heart, express your love for each other. (I love Dad's cooking, I love Mom's laugh, I love Nicole's hugs, etc.)

*Deliver Oversized Valentines

Make giant-sized valentines from poster board and take them to convalescent homes. (Big print makes reading easier.)

*Serve Breakfast in Bed

This is one day you can indulge. Go for all the yummies you like.

*Invest in a "You Are Special" Plate

And use it, even for yourself!

*Give a Jar of Love

Cut small pink and red hearts out of construction paper. Write a different, but genuine, compliment on each one. Pour them into a jar and invite someone you love to read them whenever they're blue.

*Make a Love Puzzle

Write a loving message on a large cardboard heart. Now cut it into jigsaw pieces and let a youngster assemble it.

*Write on Bananas

Give someone you love a fun lunch box surprise. Write "I love you" with a dull pencil on a banana skin. It won't show at first, but within an hour or two, your secret message will become visible.

*Cut Heart-Shaped Sandwiches

Use scissors or a heart-shaped cookie cutter.

*Stir Red Cinnamon Candies into Applesauce

Stir the mixture in a saucepan over medium heat, and the applesauce will turn a festive pink. You can also stir cinnamon candies into oatmeal, puddings, hot apple cider—be adventurous!

*Bake a Bright Red Cake

Here's the recipe for Red Velvet Cake. It's great for the Fourth of July and Christmas, too, as this cake comes out a fantastic bright red!

2 oz. red food coloring

2 Tbsp. cocoa

1 tsp. baking soda

1 tsp. vinegar

½ cup butter

1½ cup sugar

2 eggs

1 cup buttermilk

1 tsp. salt

1 tsp. vanilla

2½ cups all-purpose flour

*Preheat oven to 350°F. Make a paste of red food coloring and cocoa. Set aside. Stir together baking soda and vinegar. Set aside. Now cream butter with sugar. Add eggs, buttermilk, salt, vanilla, and red cocoa paste. Add flour to butter mixture. Beat all together. Stir in soda-vinegar mixture. **Do not beat.** Pour batter into greased and floured cake pans and bake 25–30 minutes. Frost with white or cream cheese frosting.*

FOR THE PARENTS

*Write Love Letters

Write one to your children!

*Prepare an Emergency Kit

In various areas of the country, kids are required at school to have earthquake or hurricane kits, filled with enough food and clothing to last a day in case disaster strikes and they can't be immediately rescued. Whether your area is prone to earthquakes, floods, tornadoes, or fires, it's a good idea to have an emergency kit handy (even a gas leak can require evacuation). Put your kits in backpacks you can grab on the run. Include candles and matches, a flashlight, a solar blanket, a can opener, a toy, small cans of juice and meat or tuna, other snacks, a change of clothes, cash, and first-aid items. At the end of the year, if you haven't had to use yours, celebrate by gobbling up the goodies inside.

*Rock Babies Awake

We all know you can rock a baby to soothe it to sleep. But did you know you can also ease the waking up transition for little ones? One of our sons had a hard time waking, and I found that if I let him wake up slowly, rocking him with gentle lullabies, he was able to face the day with a brighter outlook and more energy. (Gradually, the songs became more upbeat, until he was wide awake.)

*Think Ahead

Right after Christmas is the perfect time to be thinking about next Christmas. If you get into the habit of organizing, you won't be too exhausted and sick of the holidays to feel some excitement in planning the next one! This is the time to buy Christmas paper, cards, ornaments, and even Christmas fabrics for making pillowcases, oversized napkins, and tablecloths (great gifts for next year). Buy kids' turtlenecks, jackets, gloves, and boots in advanced sizes for next winter. You'll save not only money, but time and hassle when everyone else is trying to find a parking space next December!

*Begin the New Year Right

Establish an organized system for recycling. Have separate bins for plastic, newspapers, magazines, glass, aluminum, etc. Let the whole family build a compost container and learn how to use one. Before you throw anything away, ask yourself if it couldn't have just one more use.

INDEX

Joni Hilton earned a Master of Fine Arts degree in Professional Writing from the University of Southern California. She frequently shares her ideas for family fun on radio and television programs. Her writing appears in *Family Circle, Parents, Better Home & Gardens, Good Housekeeping, McCall's,* and many other publications. She is the author of ten books, including *Five-Minute Miracles: 373 Quick Daily Projects for You and Your Kids to Share.* She hosted her own daily TV show in Los Angeles for four years and is also a former news anchor. She was Miss California and a finalist in the Miss USA–Universe Pageant. Joni and her husband, Bob Hilton, live in California with their children, Richie, Brandon, Cassidy, and Nicole.